DATE DUE

THE RETURN OF PAHANA

Taiowa is the breath;
humankind, the mouthpiece
to carry the sounds of creation to
the far reaches of eternity.

Hopi Song of Creation

THE RETURN OF
PAHANA

A HOPI MYTH

Robert Boissière

foreword by Hunbatz Men
and
introduction by Barbara Hand Clow

BEAR & COMPANY
PUBLISHING
SANTA FE, NEW MEXICO

LIBRARY OF CONGRESS CATALOGING-IN-PUBLICATION DATA

Boissière, Robert, 1914-
    The return of Pahana: a Hopi myth / by Robert Boissière
       p.   cm.
    ISBN 0-939680-73-4
    1. Hopi Indians—Religion and mythology. 2. Mayas—Religion and mythology. 3. Indians—Religion and mythology. 4. Second Advent—Comparative studies. I. Title.

E99.H7B64 1990
299'.784—dc20   90-37983
                                         CIP

Bear & Company, Inc.
Santa Fe, NM 87504-2860

Cover illustration: Suzanne de Veuve © 1990, courtesy of
Floating Lotus Gallery, San Francisco
Author photo: Anders Holmquist © 1990.
Interior illustration: Angela C. Werneke © 1990
Cover & interior design: Angela C. Werneke
Editing: Barbara Doern Drew
Typography: Casa Sin Nombre, Ltd.
Printed in the United States of America by R.R. Donnelley

9 8 7 6 5 4 3 2 1

*To the future generations of young men and women
who will be witnessing and participating in the rebirth
of planet Earth.*

C O N T E N T S

P R E F A C E &
A C K N O W L E D G M E N T S

In the great mystery of life, many a negative event eventually has a positive effect. What follows has been written in the belief that many of the sufferings of humanity herald times of great and positive change — change that has been prophesied throughout the ages.

Today we are confronted with the end of an old age and the beginning of a new one. The challenge is enormous. How can we understand these tumultuous times? How can we cross the bridge between the old and the new? More importantly, how can we think and act so that our lives will be in harmony with the new world that is slowly emerging?

Throughout this book, it has been my earnest desire to shed some light on these questions — if not to relieve some of humanity's suffering, then at least to put it into perspective. For only with a healthy perspective, I believe, will the collective consciousness of humanity be inspired to transform itself and assume its rightful role in the dawning New Age.

I would like to thank all my Hopi friends, without whom this book would not have been possible. Especially the late Leslie Koyawena, who opened his home and family so I could learn the Hopi Way — he truly was my brother.

Leslie's son, Walter, as well as my dear friend Ferrell Secakuku were also a great help in my learning the Hopi Way and in discovering its Mayan connections.

I am especially thankful to Myla, my beloved companion, for her patience in listening to endless readings of rough drafts.

My thanks also to Brandt Morgan, the wise and expert editor who fine-tuned the work as it progressed.

I also want to thank Hunbatz Men, the Mayan elder and teacher who invited me to join his group of pilgrims in an unforgettable journey to the Mayan sacred centers in the Yucatán, helping me to find confirmation that there is, indeed, a Hopi-Mayan connection.

Finally, I want to express my gratitude to Gerry and Barbara Clow, my publishers, for giving me the opportunity to add to this book my "Messages for the Year 2000," which I hope will be a worthwhile contribution to the understanding of the human condition.

May all this help given me so bountifully be one more reason to believe in the beauty of the human destiny.

F O R E W O R D

The indigenous Hopi are heirs to the ancient cultural tradition of the American continent. When they perform their rituals and ceremonies, they activate the magical knowledge that has united them with their ancestors. Their rituals and dances reveal an awakening of genetic information that unites us with Mother Earth.

In a very remote time the Hopi learned how to communicate with the Great Spirit of all that surrounded them. This knowledge has supported them in their life on the mesas far from the corruption of modern civilization. Hopi time follows its destined sacred road for the Great Spirit, and in this new age of Aquarius, there is no alien influence that separates it from its cosmic destiny.

The dances and rituals of the kachinas were given to the Hopi by the spirit of their ancestors so they would remain united before the law of the universe. This was during a period when time was not kept. The indigenous Hopi know that in each kachina their ancestors are reincarnated in the new sky so they can tell their pueblo about the glorious past knowledge that can orient modern humanity.

The indigenous Hopi and Maya are very ancient on this continent. It has been thousands of years since the Hopi lived in Nah Chan, Chiapas, Mexico. We Maya are the enlightened ones in the understanding of dances and rituals that create vibrations in Mother Earth. In an unnamed cycle of time through designs of the Great Spirit, our Hopi brothers had to emigrate to the north to complete their destiny as bearers of peace in the lands of North America.

As prophecies are now being fulfilled, we see this book appear, *The Return of Pahana* by Robert Boissière. For us Maya, the Pahana is Kukulcan—two different names that represent the same symbol. The prophecies say that when the sacred symbols are newly understood, it will be the time of awakening for the human race before our father, the Sun, and his sisters, the stars.

Hunbatz Men
Mérida, Yucatán, Mexico
January 1990

Hunbatz Men, author of Secrets of Mayan Science/Religion,
*is a Mayan daykeeper, artist, and authority on the history, chronology,
and calendars of Mayan civilization.*

INTRODUCTION

Robert Boissière is a man who lives a myth, the myth of the Banana Clan, a clan of non-Hopi living in the Rio Grande Valley of New Mexico, who are inspired to live Hopi ways. For Robert, this myth began in 1948 at Hopi, Second Mesa, when a great being, Somiviki, appeared to him in a vision and said, "I have come to tell you that you will have your own clan. It will be called the Banana Clan."[1] This meant that Robert would form a clan—a group led by a vision. But its symbol was to be bananas!

What does it mean to live a myth? Myth is story that is archetypal and recurrent. Its life is based solely on belief because it has no objective reality, and it is created when people respond to story. So, to live a myth means to believe in and act out a vision or story. Mayan teacher Hunbatz Men says that myth is genetic information that unites us with the Earth and that the Hopi are heir to this cultural information. In *The Return of Pahana*, Robert says the Hopi are a microcosm of indigenous people of this planet and that they believe they are the repository of the initial instructions given to humanity by its maker. If the Hopi are correct, their knowledge is the essential guidance we need at this critical phase of evolution. It is time to understand the Hopi myth of "the return of Pahana," the return of the wandering brother.

According to Robert, when one believes in a myth, one becomes a part of it. The Banana Clan has become a part of this archetypal process by believing in the myth that began in 1948. Anthropologist Claude Levi-Straus said any myth consists of all versions, from the earliest to the latest.[2] This emphasis on essential meaning in the myth that moves beyond its historical source or culture places profound importance on the mythological teaching itself. Using this approach, myth is understood to be real only when its power is felt by individuals who respond to it. Myth is outside of chronological time. It exists in "soul time," and those individuals who are able to live it move into dimensions beyond chronological time where the genetic codes of planetary life are accessible.

To really understand Robert Boissière, we must examine the life that has led him to be clan leader, "Kikmongwi," of the Banana Clan. We must also explore the revelations that resulted from his experiences during the "Mayan Initiatic Journeys" of 1989 at the time of the spring equinox, which resulted in the Mayan and Banana Clan connection of August 1989 at Hopi. It was only then that Robert and other Bananas, including myself, saw why our totem—connecting symbol—is the banana. And that is exactly why I admire Robert. His delight in life and his sense of humor are what enabled him to believe in our myth from 1948 to 1989 without even knowing the meaning of the central symbol. He persevered because of the rich gifts the Hopi gave him when he lived with them following the Second World War. In those days, he says he felt caught in a vise that squeezed the nonessential out of him: "From a Frenchman raised in the sophistication of Parisian life, I was emerging into a world of Hopi values. Everything I was getting now was from Mother Earth."[3]

Robert's deepest knowledge comes from his life with the Hopi and his years of living at Taos pueblo with his Indian wife, Mary. These stories are available in his book *Po Pai Mo: The Search for White Buffalo Woman*. As I attempt to convey the nature of a person who is one of my spiritual teachers, I wonder about the person I read about in *Po Pai Mo* and the person I know now thirty years later. *Po Pai Mo* is a story of the search for the Goddess, and *The Return of Pahana* is the search for the return of a transcendent being imaged primarily as male. However, with Mayan medicine man Hunbatz Men in 1989 at Ux Mal, Campeche, Mexico, we were taught to fuse male and female energies, an integration that may be a more realistic image of Pahana for our time. We may miss the Messiah again as we did two thousand years ago if we have a preordained image of it.

Robert Boissière is the elder of the Banana Clan, and we can best understand the sources of wisdom he offers us by examining the phases of his life. We look to his search for the Goddess in his younger years; his exploration of prophetic skills from about 1973 to 1989, mainly reported upon in *The Return of Pahana*; and, lastly, his revelation of how fusion between male warrior gifts and female receptive wisdom is the key to planetary balance, the ceremonial fusion that we experienced during the Mayan Initiatic Journeys of 1989.

Po Pai Mo is a love story by a man who finds the Goddess. In this case, Mary of Taos Pueblo was there for Robert when he needed to discover the rare esoteric initiation that we can experience only on this planet: illumination in ordinary reality. Through the exquisite and ordinary village life combined with the other-worldly ceremonial cycle of Hopi and Taos, Robert lived the Earth/sky fusion that indigenous people live. However, Mary gave him the teaching in a personal way by completely sharing herself with him until she died a tragic early death. Mary's gift was the eternal love that any woman can offer any man, but Mary was also one of the great visionaries of this century because she helped bring the Goddess to the pueblos of New Mexico.

New Mexico is the land of the uneasy alliance, a rich blend of Native American, Hispanic, and Anglo cultures. We are blessed with the joy of many Native American clans that were never driven off their ancestral lands. I cannot live anywhere else in this country because wherever I go, I hear the cries of the tribal spirits longing for the connection to their ancestors' bones dumped in countless museum drawers. Also, we have the culture of the heart, cruel as well as loving, from our original strain of European Catholicism from the Spanish conquistadors. Unlike most of the rest of North America, here the indigenous people survived the cruel assaults of their conquerors in the early sixteenth century. Then, in 1531, on a hill in Mexico sacred to an Aztec goddess, the apparition of the Virgin Mary appeared as a dark, indigenous goddess in a blue-starred robe. In spite of the cruelties of the Roman Catholic church, the indigenous people of the Americas received the Goddess. That appearance of the Virgin of Guadalupe in Mexico signaled the beginning of the return of the Great Goddess, and the patriarchal church has had to tolerate her worship for more than four hundred years, since that was the only way the church could get power in Mexico.

Mary of Taos Pueblo recognized the Goddess in the Virgin of Guadalupe, and then she was able to connect the pueblos to this powerful force. In the mid-1950s, under Mary's guidance, dancers from Taos, San Juan, Tesuque, Santo Domingo, Santa Clara, and Cochiti pueblos traveled to Scottsdale, Arizona, to perform "The Miracle of the Roses," a reenactment of the Guadalupe mystery story.[4] To this day, the Banana Clan fuses the Hopi and Rio Grande Pueblo traditions with that of the Virgin of Guadalupe. Mary helped Robert see and feel the Goddess as a woman does, which is something given to few men.

In *The Return of Pahana*, Robert examines the Hopi myth of the return of the wandering brother, Pahana, and compares it with stories found in many cultures of the return of a great teacher who comes when humanity is in crisis. Pahana was one of two sons of a Bow Clan chief who discovered evil and disappeared into darkness. As a result, the two brothers separated, the younger to lead the Hopi in search of Maasauu, the god-guardian of the Earth, who had given them stone tablets containing the Hopi laws for living. The elder brother, Pahana, was to travel eastward to the rising sun, taking a piece of the original tablets with him. He was to return when he heard his younger brother cry out for help.

The Hopi elders consult the tablets to this day and await Pahana's return with the missing piece. I cannot help but feel that these tablets are like the Mosaic tablets, since the Hopi say Maasauu gave them the tablets with instructions on how to live. But it is interesting that the Hopi actually *have* the tablets, with the exception of the missing piece. The myth says that Pahana will come when it is time to restore balance to the world and that "he" will carry this missing piece.

The stories of the Hopi and their migrations to the four directions have always carried me thousands of year back in time to the ancient conflicts between wandering nomads and agricultural communities in the Near East. The Hopi mesas look like a Nimrud or Ur rising in the desert of the Southwest, but the Hopi ancestral lands are still inhabited by Hopi, while the Sumerian tells are mounds of earth containing the remains of ancient cities. The missing piece of the tablet offers rich metaphors, and it does not have to be understood in a literal way. Robert speculates that Harmonic Convergence on August 16-17, 1987, was a trigger event that catalyzed the morphogenetic field of humanity into spontaneous initiation of a new world order, a concept of a return to balance similar to that of the Hopi vision.

The neolithic mind—numinous, intuitive, mythic seer mind—was developed from about 25,000 B.C. to 1500 B.C., and the global mind—all-embracing consciousness of every place on the Earth—was developed from 1500 B.C. to the present time. Now we are in the midst of the reemergence of the neolithic mind into global consciousness, which will birth the planetary mind—feeling the aliveness of the Earth as in neolithic mind, while being aware of the whole planet. For me, Pahana's wandering the planet and carrying the missing piece of the Creator's laws is a metaphor for the loss of the powers of the neolithic mind. This also could be seen as a myth for the time when humankind left the primordial Garden.

The Hopi myth of Pahana is incredibly rich, because the Hopi hint that Pahana forgot the teachings during his long journey east. But he will remember the ancient laws of the stone tablets held by his Hopi clan members at exactly the right time. It is similar to the moment when a caterpillar remembers it is to become a butterfly. Like the Hopi, pushed into a small corner while the planet explodes in greed, the caterpillar grows to a point of being squashed in its chrysalis and then transmutes to a new form. The Hopi will recognize their long-lost brother because he will have the ancient wisdom, plus a new awareness from his wanderings about the globe. But it is always very clear that Pahana can return only when he *remembers* the original connection with Hopi. Always true to the myth, the Hopi live in the eternal present and do not need to judge the return. They simply wait for it to find itself. This is exactly how we will birth the planetary mind: we will remember our ancient wisdom in light of what we have learned while exploring the global mind.

What will Pahana be? Robert speculates that it might be an individual, a group of people inspired by the "light," or that it might have something to do with the yearning by feminists for the return of the Goddess. Robert also explores various myths of twins, such as Quetzalcoatl and Tezcatlipoca of the Mayan/Aztec cultures, Horus and Seth from Egypt, and the twins of the Hopi Bow Clan. He notes that musician Jim Berenholz, who is fascinated by Quetzalcoatl, envisions the return as a joining of both sides of the duality of the twin figures into harmonious balance.

That is close to how I image it, and I feel that "the world out of balance" we live with now is a sign that we are ready to accept our other piece—our shadow. The reason we developed the global brain was so we could see the shadow—the unseen parts of ourselves that have power. That is why Pahana left in the first place. Dan Katchongva of Hotevilla says that even in the 1970s the Hopi themselves did not know the significance of the Bow Clan chief's defection to the Earth center, where people from all nations meet to plan the future, but the Hopi knew it had to do with the future. In his remarkable text in chapter 2, Dan shows that the original split between the twins of the Bow Clan occurred after their father tasted evil. In other words, the defection may be the Hopi story of leaving the Garden as humankind attempts to grasp evil. It is also a story of the individual's resolution of duality or resolution by the whole group mind. The return is actually a self-knowing that comes when one has seen enough. It is wordless, just like the quietude of the Hopi. They laugh more than they talk because they delight in this world.

All that is left is the timing of the return, and this is where Hunbatz Men and Harmonic Convergence fit into the picture. Harmonic Convergence was a worldwide gathering of people at various sacred sites that was triggered by the publication in 1987 of *The Mayan Factor: Path Beyond Technology* by Dr. José Argüelles.[5] Dr. Argüelles explores a critical synthesis of time and meaning from the Aztec and Mayan calendars that catalyzed Harmonic Convergence. Remember, as Robert says, what makes a myth real is whether one believes it or not. In other words, a core group of people who believe it is time for a myth to unfold can actually trigger events!

Those of us who live in the Rio Grande Valley are fortunate that we can attend rain dances and *see* the pueblo dancers and medicine people make rain in a cloudless sky. Leslie Koyawena, a Hopi "brother" of Robert's, asked him to shoot an arrow to the sun on a cloudy but dry day so he could have rain for his cornfield. Robert sent an arrow to the sun that never returned, but the cloud darkened in three or four minutes, and the rain came down.[6] Needless to say, since Pahana was from the Bow Clan, Leslie Koyawena must have been quite amazed by Robert's feat. This is the level of childlike wonder that for so long fueled the unfoldment of the story of the Banana Clan. Then, the planetary trigger event happened in 1987 with Harmonic Convergence, and the story continues to unfold through the "Mayan Initiatic Openings—1987-1992," a project to open Mayan sacred sites led by

Hunbatz Men and other Mesoamerican medicine people.

Much of what goes on in the Banana Clan is secret and will always remain so. The myth can be seen first only in the dark night of secret ceremony. But the exoteric teaching of the Banana Clan can be known. We believe that the Earth is sacred and alive. Our members work to enliven our sense of the sacred, and we learn what we can of Hopi wisdom, Rio Grande Pueblo tradition, and the meaning of the appearance of the Virgin of Guadalupe. We believe that we are blessed to live in a place where the sense of the sacred is still alive, and we travel around the world to feed other sacred sites with prayer feathers and participate in sacred ceremony. Long before Harmonic Convergence, Bananas were quietly awakening the Earth power points, the sacred sites. As we went about our work, few of us knew about the coming convergence point in August of 1987, even though a great teacher about Mayan timing, Sioux flute player Tony Shearer, named the date of the convergence in his 1971 publication of *Lord of the Dawn, Quetzalcoatl.*[7] The convergence simply meant that a critical mass of people who knew the Earth was alive would help the Mother remember her power by stimulating her power points.

Harmonic Convergence greatly catalyzed many Bananas and indigenous people all over the planet. But for the Banana Clan, the catalyzing event that combined the "now" with the myth occurred during the 1989 spring equinox in Mexico. Robert describes these ceremonies in the Epilogue, and notes that we realized that the Mayan temple at Palenque is actually the southern source land of the Hopi. And it is filled with bananas— we had finally found the meaning of our symbol! The word *banana* is very close to Pahana, or Bahana, the Hopi brother who returns to create harmony again. In other words, by fully remembering the roots of our symbol—by finding our missing piece—we are Pahana, here to help restore balance on the planet, as are all who find the missing piece to their true identity and purpose.

The Hopi are *home*, the keepers of sacred place on Earth. Even though their land is very small, in their migrations they blessed all the lands of the Americas. They are the center of all our motion. The Maya are *time*, the calendar keepers, the daykeepers. They are the ones who tell us when the time has come. A deep vibration sounded in my body when the harbinger, the conch shell, was sounded at Hopi as the

Mayan/Banana/Hopi connection was solidified in the summer of 1989, an event also described by Robert in the Epilogue.

Harmonic Convergence and the arrival of the Maya have moved us into synchronistic time. This means that the shifts, the evolution, the actual events that are now changing our reality can be observed only by watching the connections between things. The point is, whether your favorite fruit is apples or bananas, the Garden is being remembered. After eating of the fruit of knowledge, we are reawakening the neolithic numinous mind. Hunbatz Men says in his foreword to this book, "The prophecies say that when the sacred symbols are newly understood, it will be the time of awakening for the human race before our father, the Sun, and his sisters, the stars."

Robert Boissière is a man of vision. He saw the need to reawaken the sacred by being willing to weave a myth, in this case the myth of the Banana Clan. In *The Return of Pahana*, he points the way for all of us to remember, for all of us to reclaim the deepest part of ourselves.

Barbara Hand Clow
Santa Fe, New Mexico
Spring Equinox 1990

Barbara Hand Clow is the author of Eye of the Centaur: A Visionary Guide into Past Lives, Chiron: Rainbow Bridge between the Inner and Outer Planets, *and* Heart of the Christos: Starseeding from the Pleiades. *She is priestess and teacher of the New Moon Lodge of the Banana Clan.*

NOTES

1. *Robert Boissière,* Po Pai Mo: The Search for White Buffalo Woman *(Santa Fe: Sunstone Press, 1983),* 40.
2. *Claude Levi-Strauss,* The Savage Mind *(Chicago: University of Chicago Press, 1966),* 11.
3. *Boissière,* Po Pai Mo, 38.
4. *Ibid.,* 81.
5. *José Argüelles,* The Mayan Factor: Path Beyond Technology *(Santa Fe: Bear & Company, 1987).*
6. *Boissière,* Po Pai Mo, 41.
7. *Tony Shearer,* Lord of the Dawn, Quetzalcoatl: Great Prophecies of Ancient Mexico *(Happy Camp, CA: Naturegraph Publishers, 1971),* 184.

P R O L O G U E

Chief Seattle Address

In 1854, the "Great White Chief" in Washington, President Franklin Pierce, made an offer for a large area of Indian land and promised a "reservation" for the Indian people. Chief Seathl (Seattle), chief of the Suquamish and other Salish tribes of the Pacific Northwest, replied to President Pierce, giving an address that is now considered to be one of the most beautiful and profound environmental statements ever made.[1] In it are many of the hallmarks of the dawning New Age. It also includes an eloquent prescription for the kind of attitudes and actions that will result in humanity's healthy relationship to the Earth in the years ahead.

How can you buy or sell the sky, the warmth of the land? The idea is strange to us.

If we do not own the freshness of the air and the sparkle of the water, how can you buy them?

Every part of this earth is sacred to my people. Every shining pine needle, every sandy shore, every mist in the dark woods, every clearing and humming insect is holy in the memory and experience of my people. The sap which courses through the trees carries the memories of the red man.

The white man's dead forget the country of their birth when they go to walk among the stars. Our dead never forget this beautiful earth, for it is the mother of the red man. We are part of the earth and it is part of us. The perfumed flowers are our sisters; the deer, the horse, the great eagle—these are our brothers. The rocky crests, the juices in the meadows, the body heat of the pony, and man—all belong to the same family.

So, when the Great Chief in Washington sends word that he wishes to buy our land, he asks much of us. The Great Chief sends word he will reserve us a place so that we can live comfortably to ourselves. He will be our father and we will be his children. So we will consider your offer to buy our land. But it will not be easy. For this land is sacred to us.

This shining water that moves in the streams and rivers is not just water but the blood of our ancestors. Remember that it is sacred, and teach your children that it is sacred and that each ghostly reflection in the clear water of the lakes tells of events and memories in the life of my people. The water's murmur is the voice of my father's father.

The rivers are our brothers—they quench our thirst. The rivers carry our canoes and feed our children. Remember, and teach your children, that the rivers are our brothers and yours, and give the rivers the kindness you would give any brother.

We know that the white man does not understand our ways. One portion of the land is the same to him as the next, for he is a stranger who comes in the night and takes from the land whatever he needs. The earth is not his brother, but his enemy, and when he has conquered it, he moves on. He leaves his father's grave behind, and he does not care. He kidnaps the earth from his children, and he does not care. His father's grave and his children's birthright are forgotten. He treats his mother, the earth, and his brother, the sky, as things to be bought, plundered, sold like sheep or bright beads. His appetite will devour the earth and leave behind only a desert.

I do not know. Our ways are different from your ways. The sight of your cities pains the eyes of the red man. But perhaps it is because the red man is a savage and does not understand.

There is no quiet place in the white man's cities. No place to hear the unfurling of leaves in spring, or the rustle of an insect's wings. But perhaps it is because I am a savage and do not understand. The clatter only seems to insult the ears. And what is there to life if a man cannot hear the lonely cry of the whippoorwill or the arguments of the frogs around a pool at night? I am a red man and do not understand. The Indian prefers the soft sound of the wind darting over the face of a pond, and the smell of the wind itself, cleansed by a mid-day rain, or scented with the piñon pine.

The air is precious, for all things share the same breath. The beast, the tree, the man—they share the same breath. The white man does not seem to notice the air he breathes. Like a man dying for many days, he is numb to the stench. But if we sell you our land, you must remember that the air is precious to us, that the air shares its spirit with all the life it supports. The wind that gave our grandfather his first breath also receives his last sigh. And if we sell you our land, you must keep it apart and sacred, as a place where even the white man can go to taste the wind that is sweetened by the meadow's flowers.

So we will consider your offer to buy our land. If we decide to accept, I will make one condition: The white man must treat the beasts of this land as his brothers.

I am a savage and I do not understand any other way. I have seen a thousand rotting buffaloes on the prairie, left by the white man who shot them from a passing train. I am a savage and I do not understand how the smoking iron horse can be more important than the buffalo that we kill only to stay alive.

What is man without the beasts? If all the beasts were gone, man would die from a great loneliness of spirit. For whatever happens to the beasts, soon happens to man. All things are connected.

You must teach your children that the ground beneath their feet is the ashes of our grandfathers. So that they will respect the land, tell your children that the earth is rich with the lives of our kin. Teach your children what we have taught our children, that the earth is our mother. Whatever befalls the earth befalls the sons of the earth. If men spit upon the ground they spit upon themselves.

This we know: The earth does not belong to man; man belongs to the earth. This we know. All things are connected like the blood which unites one family. All things are connected.

Whatever befalls the earth befalls the sons of the earth. Man did not weave the web of life; he is merely a strand in it. Whatever he does to the web, he does to himself.

Even the white man, whose God walks and talks with him as friend to friend, cannot be exempt from the common destiny. We may be brothers after all. We shall see. One thing we know, which the white man may one day discover: Our God is the same God. You may think now that you own Him as you wish to own our land; but you cannot. He is the God of man, and His compassion is equal for the red man and the white. This earth is precious to Him, and to harm the earth is to heap contempt on its Creator. The whites too shall pass; perhaps sooner than all other tribes. Contaminate your bed, and you will one night suffocate in your own waste.

But in your perishing you will shine brightly, fired by the strength of the God who brought you to this land and for some special purpose gave you dominion over this land and over the red man. That destiny is a mystery to us, for we do not understand when the buffalo are all slaughtered, the wild horses are tamed, the secret corners of the forest heavy with the scent of many men, and the view of the ripe hills blotted by talking wires.

Where is the thicket? Gone.

Where is the eagle? Gone.

The end of living and the beginning of survival.

THE RETURN OF
PAHANA

*"All I have is
my planting stick and my corn.
If you are willing to live
as I do,
you may live here
with me."*

(Instructions given to
the ancestors of the present-day Hopi
by Maasauu, god of the underworld
in charge of the Earth)

AUTHOR'S INTRODUCTION

The concept of a divine entity either dying or disappearing and prophesying its return in time of dire need is as old as humanity itself. In its Christian format, this concept is called the Second Coming of Christ. As a universal myth, though, it has lived in the subconscious of humanity since the beginning of time. It also has revealed itself in many different forms. The Hopi Indians of Arizona call their myth the return of Pahana.

"Pahana," or "Bahanna," is the name given by the Hopi to the mythic brother of an original pair of twins whose role was to insure harmony in the world. Pahana, who was of white coloration (the word also means "white man"), decided to leave the original people to investigate the rest of the world. He headed east. As a sort of passport, he took with him a portion of an original stone tablet that had been given to the Hopi by Maasauu, the god-guardian of the Earth.

To this day, neither Pahana nor the tablet have returned. However, Hopi myth predicts that Pahana will return bearing the stone tablet when his power is needed to reestablish balance and harmony in the world. Furthermore, the Hopi believe that this time is imminent, just as fundamentalist Christians believe the Second Coming is imminent.

The point I want to make initially is that the myth of Pahana and the Second Coming are not unrelated. They are two relatively modern myths that echo much more ancient ones—specifically, myths inspired by the periodic disappearance of the sun during every equinox, sunset, and eclipse.

To a young humanity, the sun's disappearance foreshadowed the loss of light and heat—and ultimately a slow, frigid death. Possibly great fears about the results of the loss of the sun were developed during the Ice Ages, a time of great travail for humanity that is a relatively recent memory in geologic time. For this reason, rituals and sacrifices were made to insure its periodic return at certain times of the year.

As humanity spread and grew in knowledge, so did its spiritual understanding. Eventually, the divine status once reserved only for the Sun Father was conferred on personalities such as Isis, Osiris, Venus, Aphrodite, Quetzalcoatl (the feathered serpent of Mesoamerica), and Christ—all embodiments of spiritual light. In like manner, lavish ceremonies and festivals have been held throughout the world both to insure and to celebrate the return of the god who disappears.

For example, Christ is said to have been born a few days after the winter solstice, when the sun begins its annual reappearance on the earthly scene. He is also said to have died in Jerusalem at the time of the summer solstice, when the days are longest. Jesus reappears for only a short time and only to a few intimate friends. He also appears in a nonphysical form. His is a reenactment of the disappearing god who promises to return—a myth originally springing from the intense fears of primitive humanity at a time when their supreme god, the sun, disappeared.

In a sense, it could be said that Christianity rebaptized the ancient summer solstice festivities in order to celebrate Christ's death and resurrection. Now we celebrate Easter in the spring, as a ritual of renewal that also coincides with the returning of the sun.

More to the point, though, the Bible tells us that Christ will return to take his place at the right side of God at a time when humanity is in dire need of his return. It is the same for the Hopi with the return of Pahana. Both prophecies are contemporary manifestations of an ageless cosmic drama that made its imprint not only on the collective subconscious of mankind but also on the ritual calendars of civilizations great and small.

Little by little, the sacrificial calendar, whose original purpose was to sustain the Sun Father in his yearly cycle and to protect the future of humanity, took on a broader spiritual base. Expanded solar and lunar cycles were added to the daily and yearly cycles, bringing a more permanent security. Finally, with astounding mathematical genius, the Maya created a science that predicted cycles of change for periods of five thousand to twenty-six thousand years. One of these great Mayan cycles comes to an end in A.D. 2012.

This fact raises fascinating questions about the turmoil in which the world presently finds itself. Is there a relationship between the end of the ancient Mayan cycle and the social, economic, and environmental crises of today? Could we possibly be experiencing the death throes of an old age and the beginning of a new one? Could we truly be on the verge of a Second Coming? If so, what form will it take, and how can we prepare for it?

A growing number of people today are coming to believe that man has created a socio-technological monster that can be quelled only by the coming of the Light. It is also interesting to note that growing numbers of people in the last twenty years have been returning to ancient beliefs, rituals, and social habits that have a pre-Christian pagan character. I can conclude only that these people find a wisdom in such practices that helps them deal with today's "world out of balance," as the Hopi call it.

Of all the Mesoamerican myths that have resurfaced from the past, the Quetzalcoatl-Pahana myth of the returning savior is the most widely recognized. It not only underlies the entire esoteric and mystic past of native America, but it is also astonishingly similar to the Old World myth of the Second Coming, which had its sources in Chaldean, Sumerian, Babylonian, Assyrian, Greek, Egyptian, and Roman mythology.

Later in this book I will investigate the similarities of all these myths—in particular, the concept of twins, goddesses, god-men, and metaphysical opposites. Whether these myths involve real people or fictitious personalities, I believe they all contain an uncoded message that reaches present-day humanity from the depths of a forgotten past. These myths are all precious time capsules waiting to be decoded by seekers with a new eagerness to unravel the mysteries of life.

Personally, I believe we *are* entering a new age—a time of transformation and rebirth, if you will. I also believe that the passage from the old to the new, like any birth, will not be easy. For many people on the planet, both now and in the years ahead, it will seem as if the light has truly disappeared. We will all need uncommon strength and ingenuity to see us through these times. But most of all, I think, we will need faith. And that is really what this book is about.

I am reminded of a story that illustrates this point. A couple of years ago I had the good fortune to visit the ancient Peruvian city of Machu Picchu. In early Incan times, this city served as a huge convent for a congregation of Incan nuns called the Virgins of the Sun. During my stay, I had the opportunity to learn more about the importance of the sun in the lives of these people—in particular about the solar "disappearing act" that has been the focus of ritual concern for so many thousands of years.

One day, I was intrigued by a number of two-inch-diameter holes I had discovered in the granite at the entrance to the sun temple. (I later discovered similar holes at the Coricancha, the sun temple in Cuzco.) Unable to divine their purpose, I approached a Quechua-speaking security guard and tried to make myself understood. The exchange was not easy, but with my halting Spanish and a good deal of sign language, I picked up enough to go away satisfied.

During the winter months in Machu Picchu, the guard explained, thick clouds hover over the Andes, concealing the rays of the sun. In ancient times, this was cause for great concern among the population. People wondered whether "Inti" would ever return.

Faced with this problem, the priesthood in residence eventually came up with a novel solution. They tied a huge image of the sun—a disk of solid gold—across the entrance to the temple and bored holes in the wall. Even with a little sunlight, the disk reflected enough light to quell the fears of the faithful. In this way, "Inti" never left, and the populace felt strong and secure even in the darkest of times.

This story reconfirmed for me the power and importance of faith among native peoples of the world. Native peoples and their ancient beliefs have a great deal to teach modern society. Today more than ever we need faith in order to cope with the turmoil around us. We, too, need to string up a golden sun and chink holes in the walls. We would do well, I think, to draw on ancient symbols and the wisdom of the ages in order to magnify what little light may be left in the world—and in order to reassure ourselves that it will break through the clouds again. The Hopi Indians' myth of the returning god, I think, contains much wisdom that can help us do that.

One reason I chose to focus on the Hopi, aside from the power and beauty of the Pahana myth itself, is that they and their religion are very much alive today. Their homes are built on tall cliffs in the middle of the Arizona desert, in the American Southwest. Like an island in the midst of the American dream, they are still nourished by the myths that have lived with them since time immemorial.

The Hopi are also linked in profound ways to the ancient Aztecs, Maya, and possibly other sun-worshipping South American civilizations. Their presence in North America is a perfect opportunity to explore the significance of the myth of the returning god—a myth that may contain a universal wisdom not only for the Western Hemisphere, but for the entire modern world.

Finally, there is a purely practical reason I have chosen to focus on the Hopi—namely, that I have lived with them off and on since 1948. I know many of the Hopi personally. I have also shared ceremony with them and witnessed the power of myth in their lives. For the Hopi, the myth of the return of Pahana is not just a story that is told and retold; it is a reality that still binds them together and gives them direction, even amidst the devastating influences of modern American society.

In all their hundreds of years of wandering and throughout additional hundreds of years of life on their Arizona mesas, the Hopi have never lost their faith or their simple ways of life. It is we of the industrialized world who have lost faith, we who seem to need reassurances in the modern age, not the Hopi. While we have wandered the world and even the skies, always searching for our destiny somewhere beyond, the Hopi have stayed at home with their planting sticks and their corn, trusting in Tawa, the Sun Father, and in their own roots to the Earth. While even great civilizations such as the Maya and Incas eventually left their homes and temples, or were decimated by Spanish invasion and Catholicism, the Hopi have remained steadfast in their rituals, their faith, and their humble expectancy of the return of their savior.

There are many lessons for us in the Hopi's cultural and spiritual longevity. These lessons are written on the walls of caves and cliffs and reenacted each year in ancient kachina dances. In witnessing Hopi ceremonies and learning about their prophecies, we have a unique opportunity—not just to learn about a beautiful and unusual culture, but to discover some of our forgotten American roots that reach back unbroken more than a thousand years.

C H A P T E R 1

The Hopi:
Who Are They?

Although no discrimination should be made either for or against any particular Native American group, it is nevertheless fair to note that in recent years the Hopi have gained a considerable amount of respect and attention from the American public in general, and from the so-called New Age communities in particular. This attention has often taken the form of increased respect for the Hopi as teachers of a way of life called the Hopi Way.

I believe there has been a tendency in recent years to idealize the Hopi way of life, at times disregarding the fact that they are a people with strengths and weaknesses like any other. Nevertheless, there is a purity, an admirable attachment to the old ways, a ceremonial and ritualistic as well as social life plan that sets the Hopi apart from most present-day Native American communities. I think it is significant that they are also widely known as the "People of Peace."

There are several reasons for the present-day popularity of the People of Peace. One is the fact that the Hopi ceremonial calendar has changed very little for hundreds, perhaps thousands, of years. All it takes to realize this fact is to witness a modern ceremony in the village square or in a Hopi kiva. Hopi ceremonies speak as eloquently and powerfully today of communication with spiritual realms as do ancient petroglyphs on canyon walls.

Another reason for widespread interest in the Hopi is the fact that, unlike other Pueblo tribes of the Southwest with the exception of the Zuni in New Mexico, most of their sacred ceremonies are still open to the public. (However, secret aspects of the ceremonies are carefully guarded by the priests and clan members.)

This uncommon situation relates directly to a historic event that had great impact on Hopi life: namely, the discovery of the Hopi pueblos by the Spanish conquistador Pedro de Tovar in 1540.

Pedro de Tovar was a captain in Francisco de Coronado's invasion force. He was sent with a small company of soldiers to explore the area that is now known as Arizona. In the process, he discovered the Hopi village of Awatobi, the easternmost village of the present Hopi mesas, which now lies in ruin. The Spaniards made no attempt to contact the Hopi again until Antonio de Espejo came back to Awatobi in 1583 and learned that there were five more Hopi villages to the west.

The remarkable thing about both these encounters is that they were quite friendly. In almost every other pueblo in the Rio Grande Basin, encounters with the Spanish led to hostility, violence, and decades of repression.

As a result of negative first encounters, the religious cults in most of the Pueblo cultures operate in secrecy today. The Hopi, on the other hand, who were relatively unaffected by the Spaniards, take the same liberal attitude toward outsiders as they did more than four hundred years ago. The primary Hopi rituals that bind the villages together are held openly, whether outsiders are watching or not.

The Hopi live in ancient villages located between Winslow, Tuba City, and Window Rock in northeastern Arizona. Their reservation lies in the center of the much larger Navajo reservation. The surrounding Navajos, with a population of almost three hundred thousand, are almost twenty times more numerous than the present-day Hopi, whose population numbers around twelve thousand.

When the Navajo began to arrive in the Southwest, the Hopi and Navajo were natural enemies. The Hopi lived a sedentary life in almost inaccessible villages on top of huge cliffs, while the Navajo roamed far and wide, frequently raiding and plundering the outlying pueblos. Today, however, despite some occasional frictions, they have almost normal relations.

At one time, the Hopi occupied a much broader territory than they do now. Widely scattered ruins indicate that they once inhabited parts of Arizona, Colorado, Utah, New Mexico, and northern Mexico. After the Navajo were brought back from their internment at Fort Sumner in southern New Mexico at the beginning of this century, they reoccupied their former hunting grounds, surrounding the Hopi on all sides.

When the U.S. government finished carving up the reservation area, Hopi territory was reduced to about one-fifth its former size. But the spiritual, or mythical, territory of the Hopi remains as before, bounded by the Grand Canyon to the west, the San Francisco Peaks to the south, Window Rock to the east, and the Kaibab Mountains to the north.

The Hopi speak a Uto-Aztecan dialect, testifying to the long periods some of their many clans spent both in Aztec and Ute country during their migrations. The probability is that when Toltec, Aztec, Chichimec, and Mayan cultures began to disintegrate, some clans decided to travel north to avoid the consequences of the collapse. At least two of the Hopi main spiritual clans, or "kachinas" (also called "catsinas"), are known to have come from Central America from a legendary place referred to as Ba-lát-quah-bi, or Palátkwapi, translated as "Red City of the South" or "River Running through Red City."

Interestingly, many Aztec and Mayan pyramids, temples, and cities included structures that were stuccoed in red. Legends, myths, and songs of present-day Hopi also tell of the days when the ancestors of the People of Peace occupied large territories in the American Southwest as far south as Mexico and Central America.

These facts help to explain why I chose to use the Hopi myth of the return of Pahana as a focal point to illustrate the universal myth of the return of supernatural personalities. As we shall see, that myth is not only an integral part of the Americas but of the Indo-European continent as well.

I lived with the Hopi for different lengths of time, mostly in days before electricity and paved roads. Although they were and still are a tiny society by American standards, they have thrived for hundreds of years in a bleak desert environment. This in itself is no small accomplishment.

Life at Hopi today, with televisions, telephones, automobiles, and other modern conveniences, does not have the purity it once had. But under the surface, the attitudes and qualities that helped the Hopi survive for more than a millenium are still there. And many of those qualities spring from their powerful myths.

Not just the Hopi, but the Maya, Aztecs, Toltecs, and Incas all had their myths and prophecies about the return of a white brother. One might think that these prophecies would have helped to prepare such cultures for their eventual meeting with the white race. Nevertheless, when it finally happened, the impact was far greater and much different than any of these cultures had imagined.

In order to grasp the intense shock of that meeting, imagine what the Hopi must have felt in 1540, when Pedro de Tovar and his men first rode into Awatobi. The Hopi had never even seen a horse, much less pale-skinned men with armor and strange weapons.

Neither Pedro de Tovar nor Antonio de Espejo had been sent with aggressive intent. The purpose of their expedition was discovery. Nevertheless, the military hardware of the advancing conquistadors must have been a fearsome sight to the Indians.

From all accounts, the Hopi warriors were prepared for battle. Ironically, the Spaniards were not. After many years away from their bases in Mexico, and having found no gold among the pueblos of the Southwest, Coronado's forces were disappointed and on the verge of rebellion. They just wanted to go home.

The only thing the Hopi had was corn, squash, feathers, and clothes woven from native cotton. And that is all the mounted warriors got—not as spoils of war, but as gifts from the People of Peace. The Spaniards left as they had come, without incident.

But from the Hopi point of view, the Spaniards' arrival had a profound impact—an impact that caused deep speculation. Could these men be the long-awaited "white brother" from the east? Could they be the Pahana?

In time, it became obvious that neither the Spaniards nor the white Anglo-Saxons were the mythical Pahana. The Spaniards did not respect Hopi religion, and later the Anglos forcibly took their children away from the villages to educate them "the American way." But partly because of its destructive force, the white culture was perceived as so powerful that many of the natives began associating it with the gods of their myths. For example, white people were surnamed "Pahanas" (or "Bahannas") by the Hopi, "Pansainas" by the Taos Indians of northern New Mexico, and "Viracochas" by the Quechua-speaking Incas. All three names refer to mythical divinities.

But I believe that tendency to revere the "white man" and his technology has begun to reverse itself. Today, modern technology is as available to native peoples as it is to Hispanics and Anglos. No longer do native peoples fear or revere the "white man." And as they experience technology with its positive and negative aspects, it is no longer an unknown entity. By the same token, more and more Anglos have begun to reject technology and discover a deep and abiding wisdom in the ways of the Native Americans. This is indicated not just in the way young people are embracing the Native Americans' inherent love for the Earth, but also in their increasing interest in so-called "pagan" beliefs and ceremonies that spring from native myths.

I believe these attitudinal shifts will eventually be of great benefit to all cultures. Both modern and native cultures are currently building bridges of respect and understanding whose importance to the health of the world should not be underestimated. When the day comes that these bridges are complete, the old abyss of fear and subjugation that was dug by the conquistadors will have been safely crossed, and a new era will have arisen for all of us.

Pahana & the Tibetans

As I mentioned, the Hopi predict that Pahana will return when times are so difficult that his power is needed to reestablish balance in the world. It is also said that upon his return, Pahana will wear a red cloak and either a red or yellow hat, the color of the hat depending on whether his return is welcomed or opposed. If Pahana's return is opposed, the Hopi say, he will use his awesome power to rebalance the world—with or without human approval and cooperation.

Given the symbolic nature of the Hopi myth of the return, it is interesting to speculate on what form the Pahana might take. Will it be an actual person, an enlightened individual bearing the stone tablet as unmistakable identification? Or might the Pahana be a collective entity, a group of people inspired by a new "light," or energy, coming from the direction of the rising sun? Further, will the return be the return of respect for the female? And is the yearning by feminists for the return of the Goddess also part of this story? Only time will tell.

Currently, many who are familar with the Hopi myth of the return have begun to wonder whether the "white brother" might represent, in part, the spreading of the Buddhist dharma in the West—in particular, Tibetan Buddhism. In fact, traditional Hopi are so interested in this possibility that they have arranged several meetings with Tibetan rinpoches, or holy men, in recent years.

One of these meetings began on Christmas Day, 1976, when Ven. Gomang Hhensur Rinpoche met in long sessions with the revered late Hopi elder, Grandfather David Monongye, in a kiva in the Hopi village of Hotevilla on Third Mesa. The purpose of these meetings was to evaluate and compare the spiritual teachings of Tibetan and Hopi origin, including their foundations, rituals, myths, symbols, and prophecies.

Interestingly enough, the Tibetan Buddhists also have a myth of godly return similar to that of the Hopi Pahana. But following the more realistic approach characteristic of the Tibetan frame of mind, it teaches that the return of the Sakyamuni, the living Buddha, is insured through the reincarnation of every Tibetan lama.

In contrast, the Hopi believe that the true white brother left the group of Hopi ancestors to travel in the direction of the rising sun and would return from that direction. Because of this, the Hopi anticipated the arrival of a race of light-skinned people from the East. Amazingly, they also predicted many modern inventions that would serve as signs to indicate certain stages in the unfoldment of the ancient Hopi prophecy. They also clearly foresaw that their white visitors might lose sight of their original purpose. Steeled against disappointment, they continued to watch for the one who had not left the spiritual path and who carried the actual stone tablet with him.

Could the Tibetan Dalai Lama and his emissaries, the rinpoches and lamas he has sent to the West, possibly be a part of the Pahana's return?

In October 1982, on the occasion of the International Bookfair in Frankfurt, Germany, David Monongye, spiritual leader of the village of Hotevilla, sent a message to the Dalai Lama on behalf of all the spiritual leaders and people of his village. The following is extracted from that edited message:

> We extend our sincere blessing for the success of this occasion, and our profound thanks for your invitation to express our understanding of

life on earth, from the distant past through the days ahead of us.

We understand very well that the highest way of life can only be founded upon a spiritual basis, through loyalty to the true religion of one's own tradition. For thousands of years we Hopi have followed this guideline, and have survived to this day as proof of the truth and strength of a way of life based on spiritual forces rather than on violent forms of control.

We were given our name, Hopi, for a purpose. It means peaceful, but much more than that. It refers to the Creator's Law, and the way one lives within it. In our society, those who violate their customs, which are seen as part of the natural order, are called "Ka-hopi," meaning misbehaved, wicked or destructive. . . .

So that you may understand more about our traditional way of life, and its importance in the pattern of life on earth, we offer the following observations. If you have the opportunity to see our villages firsthand, you will be able to note the changes that have recently occurred, and decide which village will be able to last through the great changes ahead.

Religion (*we-me*) is deeply respected by the Hopi. Its secrets are closely guarded. Only members of each religious society know the details of their respective rituals. Many of these rituals are performed in the seclusion of the particular society's *kiva*, which is a ceremonial chamber built partly underground. Each ceremony fits into an annual cycle according to the seasons. All the activities, songs and dance movements involved in this cycle help keep the earth in balance, especially the weather conditions necessary for each season. Moisture and warmth in the spring and summer are most important for a good harvest, and for the health and happiness of all living things. The Hopi entrust their prayers to all people, as illustrated by the fact that they never charge admission fees to spectators, knowing that there may be a few among them who have good hearts and will be praying with them. The spectators who pray help the ceremony to bring an abundance of rain and food.

Spirituality is seen in four aspects: wisdom and knowledge (*na-vo-de*), instructions (*du-da-vo*), prophecy and warnings (*ma-kus-da-da-vo*) and the beliefs (*dup-tseu-nee*). If a person has eyes, ears and an open mind, it is possible to learn from written materials, but the best learning comes from the lips of wise elders, and from the earth and nature. Our normal process of learning has been sadly distorted by the foreign concept of learning that has been forced upon us. Still, those who are respectful and serious about understanding the natural way can see that Religion and Spirituality are the most important ingredients for a good, long life.

Spiritual Center: The Hopi speak of living at the spiritual center of the earth. They describe the earth as a spotted fawn, each spot having a certain power. What does this mean, and what is it based on? Did we explore the earth to find this out? On what do we base our claim to all the land on this continent?

To this day, the Hopi insist that the land rightfully belongs to them. Long ago, we asked the Great Spirit, personified as Maasauu, for permission to live here with him. He is the caretaker of the land. We did not encroach upon his areas as did the newcomers. He allowed us to stay as caretakers, and gave us the name "Hopi," entrusting us with the sacred stone tablet which is our title to the land. We hold this title to this land only on condition that we care for it for all people, and all living things. He also gave us a warning that if we should stray from the pattern of life he laid out for us, we shall lose the use of it.

In keeping with his instructions, we migrated to all parts of the land, leaving our houses standing, and leaving rock writings and other evidence of our presence as a symbol of our claim, and as a mysterious guardian. Thus we planted a spiritual seed at each place we rested, to reach in all directions and intertwine. The houses were always built in two or three levels. The shrines stand as a contact with their respective gods for protection.

We would stay in one place for many years, until enough food had been stored to take along on the next stage of the journey, never forgetting our mission. Some clans would travel clockwise, and others counterclockwise, keeping within a day's running distance from each other. Our destination was set before we started, at which we would meet Maasauu to receive our final instructions.

After many centuries of migration, we reached the place that is now our permanent home. Here we planted the master spiritual seed, whose roots were to join all the other roots, which would meet in this place, making the land usable. This location was originally called Sip-Oraibi, or solid foundation.

Shrines were established many miles in the four directions, not as boundary markers, but as protectors having sacred power. Those who defile these shrines, or in any way defy the powers connected with them, thus create a curse on themselves. Thus this area was prepared as a sanctuary to enable life on earth to continue. We helped complete the spiritual center by following the directions of Maasauu.

We know that Hopi land is not the only spiritual center in the world. Other places were set aside by the Creator, through those following his directions, in other lands, to serve as sanctuaries during a time of great world change in the future. Their roots will be found through ancient knowledge leading to those places.

It was foretold that in time the native people would stray from their original path, adopting foreign concepts. Their religious and spiritual values would be demolished, including the foundation. Their language, their culture and their identity will cease to exist. When this happens, a few remnants will remain who are possessed of the wisdom and knowledge of old. If they are fortunate enough, these few will gather together and put together the ancient knowledge which they remember, and go forth in search of the roots the Hopi laid out, until they find the master root.

What happens then will be a source of great happiness to all, especially those who have maintained the original way throughout the ages, who will be honored for accomplishing the impossible in spite of repression from outside forces. But if these last remnants of the ancient way are toppled, a very great purification by the forces of nature will be called for, in order to restore the plan of the Creator.

The Universal Plan is very clear, but people often shy away from facing or talking about the reality of it for fear of being labeled as doomsayers, and being dishonored among respectable people. But it is really the solution by which the Creator will put the world in order. The Hopi have no dispute with this plan, for we do not put ourselves above the Creator. We have no need to say exactly how the purification will be accomplished. The Creator has weapons of nature above and beyond the armaments that humans have built for their own self-destruction.

We Hopi are waiting, for we know that no human power can stop what the Creator has to do. Those of us who have served the destructive forces by our lifestyle will reap our just punishment for losing sight of the bright path of the Creator. No grim fate would await us had we not acted like children and played with our toys of destruction. As it is, we must face what is in store for us.

The Hopi watch closely as each stage unfolds in the pattern of world change, knowing when to take the next action according to our instructions. So when the prophesied "gourd of ashes" was dropped on Japan, in which many people perished, the Hopi acted to bring their message to the world, to warn that no show of force must be applied. We knew that any attempt to control or conquer the world would only serve to destroy the world. This is simply the reality of life. We may use this warning to our benefit or our doom as we ourselves choose.

Our prophets warned that at this point those who don't heed the warning, and use their advanced technology to achieve greater weapons and greater control over nature, would bring great harm to both land and life. These people would have no understanding, but would believe in the power of their own minds, and act as if they were some super-race. They will play the game of gaining wealth through cunning, and even treachery, using false promises in their competition for power. Who knows what they will do in their intoxicated state!

Perhaps there is still time left to reawaken the misguided and prevent disaster. We learned from our ancestors that man's actions through prayer are so powerful that they decide the future of life on earth. We can choose whether the great cycles of nature will bring forth prosperity or disaster. This power was practiced long ago, when our spiritual thoughts were one. Will this concept still work in the jet age?

Let us not be discouraged. Let us cleanse our minds of delusion. Let us rid ourselves willingly of hate, and put love within ourselves, and join together with renewed faith in our Creator, so that we may be spared the destruction that results from trusting in weapons and other devices of our own minds, and not forget the future of our children and those to come.[2]

It is my privilege to have participated in the life of the Hopi when the serenity and the simplicity of life had not yet been radically altered by the import of technology and all its electronic gadgets. This was in the late forties in the village of Shipaulovi, when dirt or sand trails were still the only way to connect with the Hopi villages. They were as isolated from the rest of the world as they could be, perched atop high mesas above the parched desert floor.

In the ruggedness and monastic simplicity of those days, small children still ran around without clothes, playing with toy bows and arrows or wooden dolls. This was part of the humility of the Hopi, who had hardly changed their way of life in centuries.

To me, a Frenchman transplanted to America little more than two years before, Hopiland was like Shangri-la—a unique opportunity to participate in a pristine way of life. I lived with a Hopi family, who accepted me as their brother. I ate corn, beans, and squash from a tablecloth spread out on the dirt floor. I ate as the Hopi ate, using three fingers instead of a fork and spoon. I slept on the roof, eight hundred feet above the desert floor, with a fifty-mile panoramic view in all directions. I sometimes imagined myself an eagle flying above the ground, joyful and free.

After the sophistication of Paris, where I had spent a good deal of my life until then, my experience at Hopi brought me back to the essentials of life. My heart was full of peace during those days. Was this a dream, I sometimes wondered, or was it the place where dream and reality meet? For me it was both, and the beautiful thing about being accepted in the native world is that it is permanent. I have returned to Hopi many times since, and in spite of the changes over the years, I am always treated as if I had never left.

Much of the Hopi Way still remains, especially in ceremonial life. Customs and society have been radically altered by the influence of American society, but Hopi culture has not been broken. For the time being, at least, it still survives.

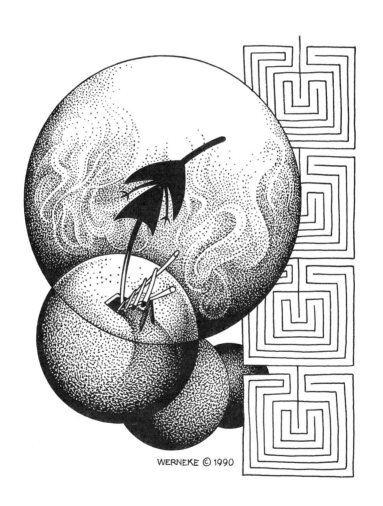

WERNEKE © 1990

The Hopi Way

In this chapter, I would like to include the text of a talk given by Hopi elder Dan Katchongva on January 29, 1970. This talk was first published by the Committee for Traditional Indian Land and Life in 1972, as a booklet entitled "From the Beginning of Life to the Day of Purification." The accuracy of the translation was carefully established by Hopi interpreter Danaqyumptewa, with emphasis given to the original wording.

This talk is an eloquent statement of the Hopi myth and mission in the modern world. I believe it is critical to understanding both the Hopi themselves and the myth of the return of Pahana.

"In this talk," says Thomas Tarbet in the booklet's introduction, "Dan told the story of the People of Peace from the dawn of time to the attacks which led to the founding of Hotevilla in 1906, the school, money and police systems which threaten to end the Hopi Way within this generation, and the consequences for America and the world.

"The thought of publishing this talk grew from the recognition that those causing this tragedy, and the millions who support them, could not persist, had they but a glimpse of the purpose behind Hopi resistance to foreign control."

Indeed, the policies of the American federal government toward the Hopi (as toward other Native Americans) have been so shocking that it is impossible to reconcile them with the ideals stated in the United States Constitution. For the Hopi, freedom of religion and respect for individual rights, customs, and education have not really existed in the last century. Over the years, they have been persecuted in regard to almost every aspect of their culture, including their lifestyle, customs, education, beliefs, and sacred rituals. As with so many native peoples, the disapproving government has often used coercion—and even armed intervention and forced deportation—to get the Hopi to submit to its plans for assimilation into the "American way."

Only in recent years has the federal government begun to see the light. And even this is more through the Hopi's own perseverance than through any official change of heart. The Hopi have always regarded themselves as the guardians of a way of life that values simplicity, purity, honesty, and, above all, humility—in short, the very values that modern humanity most needs in order to survive its present malaise. That they have managed to maintain these primary values in the face of relentless change and outside pressure is nothing less than astounding. Most of the fuel for this perseverance is contained in their core beliefs and philosophies as explained here by Dan Katchongva.

THE BEGINNING OF LIFE

Somewhere down in the underworld we were created by the Great Spirit, the Creator. We were created first one, then, two, then three. We were created equal, of oneness, living in a spiritual way, where the life is everlasting. We were happy and at peace with our fellow men. All things were plentiful, provided by our Mother Earth upon which we were placed. We did not need to plant or work to get food. Illness and troubles were unknown. For many years we lived happily and increased to great numbers.

When the Great Spirit created us, he also gave us instructions or laws to live by. We promised to live by his laws so that we would remain peaceful, using them as a guideline for living happily upon that land where he created and placed us. But from the beginning he warned us that we must not be tempted by certain things by which we might lose this perfect way of life.

Of course we had advantage of many good things in this life, so by and by we broke the Creator's command by doing what he told us not to do. So he punished us by making us as we are now, with both soul and body. He said, "From now on you will have to go on your own. You will get sick, and the length of your life will be limited."

He made our bodies of two principles, good and evil. The left side is good for it contains the heart. The right side is evil for it has no heart. The left side is awkward but wise. The right side is clever and strong, but it lacks wisdom. There would be a constant struggle between the two sides, and by our actions we would have to decide which was stronger, the evil or the good.

We lived in good ways for many years, but eventually evil proved to be stronger. Some of the people forgot or ignored the Great Spirit's laws and once again began to do things that went against his instructions. They became materialistic, inventing many things for their own gain, and not sharing things as they had in the past. This resulted in a great division, for some still wanted to follow the original instructions and live simply.

The inventive ones, clever but lacking wisdom, made many destructive things by which their lives were disrupted, and which threatened to destroy all the people. Many of the things we see today are known to have existed at that time. Finally immorality flourished. The life of the people became corrupted with social and sexual license, which swiftly involved the Kikmongwi's (chief's) wife and daughters, who rarely came home to take care of their household duties. Not only the Kikmongwi but also the high religious leaders were having the same problem. Soon the leaders and others with good hearts were worried that the life of the people was getting out of control.

The Kikmongwi gathered the high priests. They smoked and prayed for guidance toward a way to solve the corruption. Many times they gathered, until finally someone suggested that they move, find a new place, and start a new life.

EMERGENCE INTO THE PRESENT WORLD

Now, they had often heard certain thumping sounds coming from above, so they knew that someone might be living there. It was decided that this must be investigated. I will describe this briefly, for the whole story would take much space.

Being gifted with wisdom, they created birds for this purpose. I will name three. Two which are known for their strength and swiftness are the *kisa* (hawk) and the *pavowkaya* (swallow). The third was a *moochnee* (related to the mockingbird). His flight is awkward, but he is known to be wise. They were each created at separate times by magic songs, tobacco smoke and prayers, from dirt and saliva, which was covered by a white cape (*ova*). Each was welcomed respectfully and given instructions for his mission, should he succeed. The first two failed to reach the top side of the sky, but the third one, *moochnee*, came through the opening into this world.

The new world was beautiful. The Earth was green and in bloom. The bird observed all his instructions. His sense of wisdom guided him to the being he was instructed to seek. When he found him it was high noon, for the being, Maasauu, the Great Spirit, was preparing his noonday meal. Ears of corn lay beside the fire. He flew down and lit on top of his *kisi* (shady house) and sounded his arrival.

Maasauu was not surprised by the visitor, for by his wisdom and sense of smell he already knew someone was coming. Respectfully he welcomed him and invited him to sit down. The interview was brief and to the point. "Why are you here? Could it be important?" "Yes," said the *moochnee*. "I was sent here by the underworld people. They wish to come to your land and live with you, for their ways have become corrupted. With your permission they wish to move here with you and start a new life. This is why I have come." Maasauu replied bluntly, but with respect, "They may come."

With this message the bird returned to the underworld. While he was gone, the Kikmongwi and the leaders had continued to pray and wait for his successful return. Upon his return with the good news of the new world and Maasauu's permission for them to come, they were overjoyed.

Now the question was how they were to get to the top, so again they smoked and prayed for guidance. At last they agreed to plant a tree that would grow to the top and serve as a pathway. They planted the seed of a *shalavee* (spruce tree), then they prayed and sang magic songs. The tree grew and grew until it reached the sky, but its branches were so soft and so many that it bent under the heavy earth pressure from the top, so it did not pierce the sky. They planted another seed, this one to be a *louqu* (pine). It grew as they sang their magic songs. This tree was stout and strong. "Surely this one will go through," they thought. But it was unsuccessful, for its branches also bent upon contact with the solid object. Again they planted a seed. This time it was a *pakave* (reed). Since it had a pointed end it pierced the sky up into the new world.

Meanwhile, all of this had been kept secret. Only proper righteous and one-hearted people were informed of the plans to leave the corrupt world. They were prepared to move out, so as soon as they knew it was successful they started to come up on the inside of the plant, resting between the joints as they worked their way up to the opening.

When they got to this world, everything was beautiful and peaceful. The land was virgin, unmolested. They were very happy. They sang and danced with joy, but their joy was short-lived, for that night the chief's daughter died suddenly. Everyone was sad and worried. People looked at one another suspiciously. An evil spell had been enacted. This caused great concern that a witch or two-hearted person might be among them.

Now the Kikmongwi had great power which he must use to settle the concern of his people. He made a small ball out of cornmeal which he tossed up above the group of people. The one upon whose head it landed would be the guilty one. It landed upon the head of a girl. A quick decision was made to throw her back through the opening into the underworld. The wickedness must be gotten rid of, for they wished to live peacefully in this new land. But the witch girl cried out for mercy, telling them that on their long journey they would face many obstacles and dangers of every description, and that her services would become useful, for she had power to fight evil. She invited the Kikmongwi to look back down into the underworld. He looked and saw his child playing happily with the other children in the underworld, where upon death we will all return. She was spared, but they left her there alone, perhaps hoping that she would perish by some unknown cause.

THE FIRST MEETING WITH
THE GREAT SPIRIT IN THIS WORLD

It was here that the Great Spirit first appeared to them on this Earth, to give them the instructions by which they were to live and travel. They divided into groups, each with its selected leader. Before them he laid ears of corn of various lengths. They were each instructed to pick one ear of corn to take with them on their journey, for their subsistence and their livelihood. One by one they greedily picked out the longest and most perfect-looking ears until only the shortest was left. They did not realize that this was a test of wisdom. The shortest ear was picked by the humblest leader. Then the Great Spirit gave them their names and the languages by which they would be recognized. The last picker of short corn was named Hopi.

"Hopi" means not only to be peaceful, but to obey and have faith in the instructions of the Great Spirit, and not to distort any of his teachings for influence or power, or in any way to corrupt the Hopi way of life. Otherwise the name will be taken away.

He then gave them instructions according to which they were to migrate for a certain purpose to the four corners of the new land, leaving many footprints, rock writings and ruins, for in time many would forget that they were all one, united by a single purpose in coming up through the reed.

Now that we were on top, we were each to follow our own leaders, but so long as we did not forget the instructions of the Great Spirit we would be able to survive. We were now bound by a vow to live by these instructions and to complete our pattern of migration. Maasauu told us that whoever would be the first to find him would be the leader of those who were to follow; then he disappeared.

AN ACT OF PROPHETIC CONSEQUENCE

We migrated for many years to every corner of this continent, marking our claim as we traveled, as these markings clearly testify up to the present day. On our way we stopped for rest near the great river now known as the Colorado. We had traveled far and gained a great deal of knowledge, not forgetting our instructions. The group leader was of the Bow Clan, a great chief with wisdom. But it was here that this great chief disappeared into the dark night. After putting his family to sleep he left in search of the Earth Center, where clever, ingenious people from all nations meet to plan the future. By some means he found the place, and was welcomed with respect. It was a beautiful place with all manner of good things. Good food was laid before him by most beautiful girls. It was all very tempting.

Until today we did not know the significance of this action. It had to do with the future. By this action he caused a change to occur in the pattern of life as we near the end of the life cycle of this world, such that many of us would seek the materialistic world, trying to enjoy all the good things it has to offer before destroying ourselves. Those gifted with the knowledge of the sacred instructions will then live very cautiously, for they will remember and have faith in these instructions, and it will be on their shoulders that the fate of the world will rest. The people will corrupt the good ways of life, bringing about the same life as that from which we fled in the underworld. The sacred body of the female will no longer be hidden, for the shield of protection will be uplifted, an act of temptation toward sexual license, which will also be enjoyed. Most of us will be lost in all the confusion. An awareness that something extraordinary is happening will develop in most of the people, for even their leaders will be confused into polluting themselves. It will be difficult to decide whom to follow.

The Hopi knew all this would come about. All these aspects of today's life pattern were planned. So today we must stand firmly on our belief in order to survive. The only course is to follow the instructions of the Great Spirit himself.

THE MISSION OF THE TWO BROTHERS

This Bow Clan chief had two grown sons. When they learned of their father's misdeed, they were very sad. Their knowledge of the teachings which they had received from him was all in order. Now they were left alone to lead their people, for the very next day their father died.

They asked their mother to permit them to carry out the order of their instructions for an event of this nature. She replied that it was up to them, for their knowledge was complete. Upon agreement, the younger brother was to continue in search of Maasauu, and to settle where he found him. There he would await the return of his older brother, who was to travel eastward toward the rising Sun, where he would rest briefly. While resting, he must listen for the voice of his younger brother, who would expect him to come to his aid, for the change in the life pattern will have disrupted the way of life of his people. Under the pressure of a new ruler they will surely be wiped off the face of the Earth unless he comes.

So today we are still standing firmly on the Great Spirit's instructions. We will continue to look and pray toward the east for his prompt return.

The younger brother warned the elder that the land and the people would change. "But do not let your heart be troubled," he said, "for you will find us. Many will turn away from the life plan of Maasauu, but a few of us who are true to his teachings will remain in our dwellings. The ancient character of our head, the shape of our houses, the layout of our villages and the type of land upon which our village stands, and our way of life—all will be in order, by which you will find us.

Before the first people had begun their migrations the people named Hopi were given a set of stone tablets. Into these tablets the Great Spirit inscribed the laws by which the Hopi were to travel and live the good way of life, the peaceful way. They also contained a warning that the Hopi must beware, for in time they would be influenced by wicked people to forsake the life plan of Maasauu. It would not be easy to stand up against this, for it would involve many good things that would tempt many good people to forsake these laws. The Hopi would be led to a most difficult position. The stones contained instructions to be followed in such a case.

The older brother was to take one of the stone tablets with him to the rising Sun, and bring it back with him when he hears the desperate call for aid. His brother will be in a state of hopelessness and despair. His people may have forsaken the teachings, no longer respecting their elders, and even turning upon their elders to destroy their way of life. The stone tablets will be the final acknowledgement of their true identity and brotherhood. Their mother is Sun Clan. They are the children of the Sun.

So it must be a Hopi who traveled from here to the rising Sun and is waiting someplace. Therefore it is only the Hopi that still have this world rotating properly, and it is the Hopi who must be purified if this world is to be saved. No other person anyplace will accomplish this.

The older brother had to travel fast on his journey for there was not much time, so the horse was created for him. The younger brother and his people continued on in search of Maasauu.

On their way they came to a land that looked fertile and warm. Here they marked their clan symbols on the rock to claim the land. This was done by the Fire Clan, the Spider Clan, and the Snake Clan. This place is now called Moencopi. They did not settle there at that time.

While the people were migrating, Maasauu was waiting for the first ones to arrive. In those days he used to take walks near the place where he lived, carrying a bunch of violet flowers (du-kyam-see) in his belt. One day he lost them along the way. When he went to look for them he found that they had been picked up by the Hornytoad Woman. When he asked her for the flowers she refused to give them back, but instead gave him her promise that she would help him in time of need. "I too have a metal helmet," she told him (possibly meaning that certain people with metal helmets would help the Hopi when they get into difficulty).

Often Maasauu would walk about a half mile north of his du-pa-cha (a type of temporary house) to a place where there lay a long rock which formed a natural shelter, which he must have picked as the place where he and the first people would find each other. While waiting there he would amuse himself by playing a game to test his skill, the name of which (*Nadu-won-pi-kya*) was to play an important part later on in the life of the Hopi, for it was here that the knowledge and wisdom of the first people was to be tested. Until recent times children used to play a similar game there, something like "hide-and-seek." One person would hide, then signal by tapping on the rock, which would transmit the sound in a peculiar way so that the others could not tell exactly where the tapping was coming from. (Some years ago this rock was destroyed by government road builders.) It was here that they found Maasauu waiting.

MEETING WITH MAASAUU NEAR ORAIBI

Before the migrations began Maasauu had let it be known, though perhaps not by direct instructions, that whoever would find him first would be the leader there. Later it became clear that this was a procedure by which their true character would be specified.

When they found him, the people gathered and sat down with him to talk. The first thing they wanted to know was where he lived. He replied that he lived just north of there at a place called Oraibi. For a certain reason he did not name it fully. The full name is Sip-Oraibi, meaning something that has been solidified, referring to the fact that this is the place where the Earth was made solid.

They asked permission to live there with him. He did not answer directly, for within them he saw evil. "It's up to you," he said. "I have nothing here. My life is simple. All I have is my planting stick and my corn. If you are willing to live as I do, and follow my instructions, the life plan which I shall give you, you may live here with me, and take care of the land. Then you shall have a long, happy, fruitful life."

Then they asked him whether he would be their leader, thinking that thus they would be assured a peaceful life. "No," he replied, "the one who led you here will be the leader until you fulfill your pattern of life" (for he saw into their hearts and knew that they still had many selfish desires). "After that I will be the leader, but not before, for I am the first and I shall be the last." Having left all the instructions with them, he disappeared.

THE ARRIVAL OF ANOTHER RACE FORETOLD

Time passed on, people passed on, and the prophecies of things to come were passed from mouth to mouth. The stone tablets and the rock writing of the life plan were often reviewed by the elders. Fearfully they waited as they retold the prophecy that one day another race of people would appear in their midst and claim our land as his own. They would try to change our pattern of life. They would have a "sweet tongue" or a "fork tongue," and many good things by which we would be tempted. They would use force in an attempt to trap us into using weapons, but we must not fall for this trick, for then we ourselves would be brought to our knees, from which we might not be able to rise. Nor must we ever raise our hand against any nation. We now call these people *Bahanna*.

THE FORCES OF PURIFICATION

We have teachings and prophecies informing us that we must be alert for the signs and omens which will come about to give us courage and strength to stand on our beliefs. Blood will flow. Our hair and our clothing will be scattered upon the Earth. Nature will speak to us with its quakes and floods causing great disasters, changes in the seasons and in the weather, disappearance of wildlife, and famine in different forms. There will be gradual corruption and confusion among the leaders and the people all over the world, and wars will come about like powerful winds. All of this has been planned from the beginning of creation.

We will have three people standing behind us, ready to fulfill our prophecies when we get into hopeless difficulties: the *Meha Symbol* (which refers to a plant that has a long root, milky sap, grows back when cut off, and has a flower shaped like a *swastika*, symbolizing the four great forces of nature in motion), the *Sun Symbol*, and the *Red Symbol*. Bahanna's intrusion into the Hopi way of life will set the Meha Symbol in motion, so that certain people will work for the four great forces of nature (the four directions, the controlling forces, the original force) which will rock the world into war. When this happens we will know that our prophecies are coming true. We will gather strength and stand firm.

This great movement will fall, but because its subsistence is milk, and because it is controlled by the four forces of nature, it will rise again to put the world in motion, creating another war, in which both the Meha and the Sun Symbol will be at work. Then it will rest in order to rise a third time. Our prophecy foretells that the third event will be the decisive one. Our road plan foretells the outcome.

This sacred writing speaks the word of the Great Spirit. It could mean the mysterious *life seed* with two principles of tomorrow, indicating one, inside of which is two. The third and last; which will it bring forth, purification or destruction?

This third event will depend upon the Red Symbol, which will take command, setting the four forces of nature (Meha) in motion for the benefit of the Sun. When he sets these forces in motion, the whole world will shake and turn red and turn against the people who are hindering the Hopi cultural life. To all these people Purification Day will come. Humble people will run to him in search of a new world, and the equality that has been denied them. He will come unmercifully. His people will cover the Earth like red ants. We must not go outside to watch. We must stay in our houses. He will come and gather the wicked people who are hindering the red people who were here first. He will be looking for someone whom he will recognize by his way of life, or by his head (the special Hopi haircut), or by the shape of his village and his dwellings. He is the only one who will purify us.

The Purifier, commanded by the Red Symbol, with the the help of the Sun and the Meha, will weed out the wicked who have disturbed the way of life of the Hopi, the true way of life on Earth. The wicked will be beheaded and will speak no more. This will be the Purification for all righteous people, the Earth, and all living things on the Earth. The ills of the Earth will be cured. Mother Earth will bloom again and all people will unite into peace and harmony for a long time to come.

But if this does not materialize, the Hopi traditional identity will vanish due to pressure from Bahanna. Through the white man's influence, his religions, and the disappearance of our sacred land, the Hopi will be doomed. This is the Universal Plan, speaking through the Great Spirit since the dawn of time.

With this in mind, I as a Hopi do not make wars against any country, because if I do, the Purifier will find out and punish me for fighting. And since I am a Hopi, I am not sending my children across the ocean to fight. If they want to that's up to them, but they will no longer be Hopi if they do.

Since I am Sun Clan, and the Sun is the father of all living things, I love my children. If they realize what I am talking about they must help me save this world.

The Hopi have been placed on this side of the Earth to take care of the land through their ceremonial duties, just as other races of people have been placed elsewhere around the Earth to take care of her in their own ways. Together we hold the world in balance, revolving properly. If the Hopi nation vanishes, the motion of the Earth will become eccentric, the water will swallow the land, and the people will perish. Only a brother and a sister may be left to start a new life.

THE FAITHFUL HOPI MEET THEIR TEST

Bahanna came with great ambitions and generosity, eagerly offering his hand to help "improve" our way of life, establishing schools to teach us the "better ways" of his life. He offered us his medicine and health practices, saying that this would help us live longer. He offered to help us mark our boundary, claiming that in that way we would have more land. In all the villages we rejected his offer. He tried many ways to induce us, but failed to make us submit to his wishes, for we were all one unity at that time, believers in the instructions of Maasauu.

His next attempt was fear. He formed a police force consisting partly of certain people who had been tempted by his offers and given weapons. He threatened to arrest us and put us in prison, but we still stood firm. The threats of arrest and imprisonment were put into action. Villages panicked and weaker people began to submit. In Oraibi, our village leadership fell when Loloma (Bear Clan) made an agreement with the United States government.

We who still had faith in Maasauu, including the main priests of the religious orders, gathered together, rejecting the Kikmongwi's request to submit. We sat down together and smoked and prayed that we would be brave enough to take our stand. We took out our stone tablet and studied it in every detail. We carefully reviewed the road plan written on the rock near our village. This is the plan we must always follow, for it is in order and complete. We recognized that the Fire Clan (meaning my father, Yukiuma) must lead, for his symbol, Maasauu, stands to the right of the reed as he faces out. We also interpreted that since our way of life had been corrupted we must move to a new place where we would be able to follow the road without interference and continue our ceremonial duties for all beings.

We smoked and prayed again and reconsidered that this village, Oraibi, is our mother village. All our sacred shrines are rooted here and must not be left unattended. We knew that the road would be hard with many obstacles. We knew that we would still be troubled by the newcomer, and that we must still face all the tests of weakness, so we agreed to stay.

The trouble commenced its course. The government wanted all of the Hopi children to be put into schools. They said it would do us good, but we knew that this "good" would only be on the surface, and that what was under it would destroy the Hopi cultural life. Maybe they thought that with an education the children might be able to help the old people, but we knew this would not be so, because they would learn to think as white men, so they would never help the old people. Instead they would be indoctrinated and encouraged to turn against us, as they are actually doing today. So in order to be good according to the Great Spirit's instructions, we refused to put our children into the schools.

So almost every week they would send policemen, many of them. They would surround the village and hunt for the children of school age. We could not be happy because we were expecting trouble every day. Fathers who refused to cooperate were arrested and imprisoned. Inhuman acts were imposed upon us, starvation, insults and humiliation, to force us into submission. Still, over half of the clan leaders and religious society leaders refused to accept anything from the government. Because of this, we were mocked and treated as outcasts by those who had already submitted. Finally, they decided to do something about us because we were keeping them from getting certain favors from the government.

What follows gives a good indication that some of the Hopi, rather than facing harsh reprisals, opted for compromise with the intruders. In doing so, they created two distinct political factions that are still operative today: namely, the "traditionalists," who strongly resist change of any kind, and the "progressives," who have been open to the introduction of electricity, telephones, automobiles, nontraditional education, government housing, and other modern conveniences.

These two sociopolitical factions of Hopi life are still strongly delineated. The village of Hotevilla, for example, is proud of the fact that it does not allow electricity and all the "ills" that come with it, including telephone, television, and the plethora of electrical gadgets that have so changed life in the other villages. They are proud to have maintained their ancestral ways in spite of social pressures to change and conform.

Among the other villages, there are many individuals who also claim to follow the conservative ways while at the same time using modern facilities that have been installed by the Bureau of Indian Affairs. To some extent, I compare this situation to the American political philosophies, divided between Democrats and Republicans.

In spite of their often marked differences, the Hopi of different villages remain united on many fronts—especially in their strong belief in the kachina cult, the exoteric base of all their ceremonial and ritual practices.

A second area of agreement is the Hopi's almost universal ostracism of the Hopi Council, a body of nonelected Hopi representatives that deals constantly with the federal government. This body claims to represent all Hopi, but most Hopi consider it a puppet of the American government that does not deal with their real needs.

In fact, what most Hopi consider their primary need is simply to be left alone—to govern themselves according to their ancestral beliefs and the ancient lifestyle that has come to be known as the Hopi Way. Dan Katchongva's continuing narrative gives a good perspective on the development of this modern attitude.

This was when Loloma's successor, Tawaquaptewa, became chief of Oraibi. It was under his leadership that the sad event, the eviction of the faithful Hopi from Oraibi, was touched off. Since we "hostiles," as we were called by the missionaries and government workers, refused to follow his wishes and accept the white man's way of life, he decided to evict us bodily. He figured that without our interference he would be able to take advantage of the good things offered by Bahanna.

THE FAITHFUL HOPI EVICTED FROM ORAIBI

On September 7, 1906, his followers, commanded by Chief Tawaquaptewa himself, entered the house where we were discussing prophesies and threw us out. We did not resist until rifles and other weapons were shown and they began beating us. Then we resisted only to the extent of defending ourselves from injury. I was knocked unconscious. When I came to, all my people were gathered to go. My father, Yukiuma, was selected to be the leader. The women and children, with a few belongings on their backs, a little food, and no shoes, were prepared to leave.

Some tried to go back to their houses to get their valuables and some extra food, but they were turned back. (In *Book of the Hopi*, it is said we were allowed to go back to get some belongings, but this is not true. That book is not accurate.) After we had left, we learned that our houses had been looted and that horses had been turned loose in our fields and had eaten our crops, which were just ready for harvest.

Thus we had to migrate once again to find a new home, leaving behind a corrupt world of confusion. We sought to start a new life, carry on our ceremonial cycles, and preserve our way of life without interference, but now we know that this was a dead dream, for the interference has continued right up to the present day.

THE FOUNDING OF HOTEVILLA VILLAGE

The village of Hotevilla was settled for one purpose: to stand firmly on the Great Spirit's instructions and fulfill the prophecies to the end. It was established by good people, one-hearted people who were actually living these instructions. Water was plentiful, and so was wood, from which we built temporary shelters in which we were to survive the cold winter with very few blankets. Food was scarce, but we managed to live from the land by hunting game and picking greens. We were united into oneness, but it would again be split into two due to extreme pressure from the outside.

RENEWED ATTACKS

Hardly had our footprints faded away in Oraibi, when early one morning we found ourselves surrounded by government troops. All the people, including the children, were ordered to march six miles to a place below Oraibi. From there, all the men were marched over forty miles to the U.S. government agency at Keams Canyon, where they were imprisoned for about a year and one half for not accepting the generous offer of education for our children, among other things.

The first thing they ordered us to do was to sign papers. We refused. Then they locked us inside a building without food and with very little water for several days until we were very hungry. Again they tried to induce us to sign papers, promising to feed us and let us go, but again we refused. They tried other tricks to make us sign, but each time we refused. Finally they took us to a blacksmith shop, where they riveted chains to our legs with loops and hooks, and fastened us together in pairs. In this way we were forced to work on a road gang for long hours, working dangerously with dynamite on the steep rocky cliffs near the agency. That road is now the foundation of a highway still in use today.

At night we were fastened together in groups of six by means of long chains. To add to our torture, soap was added to our food, which made us very sick. When one man had to go to the outhouse, all six had to go. All this time the possibility of signing certain papers was left open to those who might weaken. During this period, my father, Yukiuma, was being held somewhere else, so I was acting as leader.

While we were in prison, only the women and children and maybe a few old men were left out here. They had very little food, but as if by a miracle, there happened to be a lot of rabbits and other wild game, so on that meat diet they were able to survive the hard winter. It was very hard while the men were away. The old people used to talk about it. The women had to gather the wood themselves. My mother used to tell me how they would form hunting parties and get the dogs to help. We had a small flock of sheep which they tended while we were away. During the growing season, they planted the crops, took care of the fields, and did all the work that the men would normally do, in order to survive.

THE DISRUPTION CONTINUES TODAY

At the present time we face the danger that we might lose our land entirely. Through the influence of the U.S. government, some people of Hopi ancestry have organized what they call the Hopi Tribal Council, patterned according to a plan devised by the government for the purpose of negotiating directly with the government and with private businesses. They claim to act in the interests of the Hopi people, despite the fact that they ignore the existing traditional leaders, and represent only a small minority of the people of Hopi blood.

Large areas of our land have been leased, and this group is now accepting compensation from the Indian Claims Commission for the use of 44,000,000 acres of Hopi land. This is in error, for we laid our aboriginal claim to all of this land long before the newcomers ever set foot upon it. We do not recognize man-made boundaries. We true Hopi are obligated to the Great Spirit never to cut up our land, nor to sell it. For this reason we have never signed any treaty or other document releasing this land. We have protested all these moves, but to no avail.

Now this Tribal Council was formed illegally, even according to white man's law's. We traditional leaders have disapproved and protested from the start. In spite of this, they have been organized and recognized by the United States government for the purpose of disguising its wrongdoings to the outside world. We do not have representatives in this organization, nor are we legally subject to their regulations and programs. We Hopi are an independent sovereign nation, by the law of the Great Spirit, but the U.S. government does not want to recognize the aboriginal leaders of this land. Instead, he recognizes only what he himself has created out of today's children in order to carry out his scheme to claim all of our land.

Because of this, we now face the greatest threat of all: the actual loss of our cornfields and gardens, our animals and wild game, and our natural water supply, which would put an end to the Hopi way of life. At the urging of the Department of the Interior, the Tribal Council has signed several leases with an outside private enterprise, the Peabody Coal Company, allowing them to explore our land for coal deposits, and to strip-mine the sacred mesas, selling the coal to several large power plants. This is part of a project intended to bring heavy industry into our area against our wishes.

We know that this will pollute the fields and grazing lands and drive out the wildlife. Great quantities of water will be pumped from beneath our desert land and used to push coal through a pipe to a power plant in another state (Nevada). The loss of this water will affect our farms as well as the grazing areas of the animals. It also threatens our sacred springs, our only natural source of water, which we have depended upon for centuries.

We Hopi knew all this would come about, because this is the Universal Plan. It was planned by the Great Spirit and the Creator that when the white man came, he would offer us many things. If we were to accept those offers from his government, that would be the doom of the Hopi nation. Hopi is the bloodline of this continent, as others are the bloodline of other continents. So if Hopi is doomed, the whole world will be destroyed. This we know, because this same thing happened in the other world. So if we want to survive, we should go back to the way we lived in the beginning, the peaceful way, and accept everything the Creator has provided for us to follow.

White man's laws are many, but mine is one. White man's laws are all stacked up. So many people have made the rules, and many of them are made every day. But my law is only the Creator's just one. And no man-made law must I follow, because it is ever-changing and will doom my people.

We know that when the time comes, the Hopi will be reduced to maybe one person, two persons, three persons. If he can withstand the pressure from the people who are against the tradition, the world might survive from destruction. We are at the stage where I must stand alone, free from impure elements. I must continue to lead my people on the road the Great Spirit made for us to travel. I do not disregard anyone. All who are faithful and confident in the Great Spirit's way are at liberty to follow the same road. We will meet many obstacles along the way. The peaceful way of life can be accomplished only by people with strong courage, and by the purification of all living things. Mother Earth's ills must be cured.

As we say, the Hopi are the first people created. They must cure the ills of their own bloodline so everything will become peaceful naturally, by the will of the Creator. He will cure the world. But right now Hopi is being hurt. To us this is a sign that the world is in trouble. All over the world they have been fighting, and it will get worse. Only purification of the Hopi from disruptive elements will settle the problems here on this Earth. We didn't suffer all this hardship and punishment for nothing. We live by these prophecies and teachings, and no matter what happens, we will not buckle down under any pressure from anybody.

We know certain people are commissioned to bring about the Purification. It is the Universal Plan from the beginning of creation, and we are looking up to them to bring purification to us. It is in the rock writings throughout the world, on different continents. We will come together if people all over the world know about it. So we urge you to spread this word around so people will know about it, and the appointed ones will hurry up with their task, to purify the Hopi and get rid of those who are hindering our way of life.

I have spoken. I wish this message to travel to all corners of this land and across the great waters, where people of understanding may consider these words of wisdom and knowledge. This I want. For people may have different opinions about some things, but because of the nature of the beliefs upon which this Hopi life is based, I expect that at least one will agree, maybe even two. If three agree, it will be worth manyfold.

I am forever looking and praying eastward to the rising Sun for my true white brother to come and purify the Hopi. My father, Yukiuma, used to tell me that I would be the one to take over as leader at this time, because I belong to the Sun Clan, the father of all the people on the Earth. I was told that I must not give in, because I am the first. The Sun is the father of all living things from the first creation. And if I am done, the Sun Clan, then there will be no living thing left on the Earth. So I have stood fast. I hope you will understand what I am trying to tell you.

I am the Sun, the father. With my warmth all things are created. You are my children, and I am very concerned about you. I hold you to protect you from harm, but my heart is sad to see you leaving my protecting arms and destroying yourselves. From the breast of your mother, the Earth, you receive your nourishment, but she is too dangerously ill to give you pure food. What will it be? Will you lift your father's heart? Will you cure your mother's ills? Or will you forsake us and leave us with sadness, to be weathered away? I don't want this world to be destroyed. If this world is saved, you all will be saved, and whoever has stood fast will complete this plan with us, so that we will all be happy in the Peaceful Way.

People everywhere must give Hopi their most serious consideration—our prophecies, our teachings, and our ceremonial duties—for if Hopi fails, it will trigger the destruction of the world and all mankind. I have spoken through the mouth of the Creator. May the Great Spirit guide you on the right path.[3]

For most readers, it is probably difficult to accept the idea that the Hopi are the guardians of world balance, without which there will be no future for the human race. But before we dismiss this view as mere ethnocentric "myth," let us remember that the Hopi, by virtue of centuries of living close to the land, live by senses that for most of us have either been lost to or severely dulled by modern civilization. No longer are most of us open to the messages contained in wind and water. No longer do we share the pangs of plants, animals, and the other sentient beings who share the planet with us. No longer do we feel the agonies of the Earth as the forests are felled and the skies fill with smoke. The Hopi still do.

In this sense, the warnings of the Hopi and other native peoples cannot be passed off so easily. Collectively, they are like the canary in the mine shaft, whose sensitivity warns the miners that the oxygen is running out. The Hopi, through their vision and prophecy, have repeatedly warned the world that time is running out, that something must be done to reverse the fatal imbalances in our environment and in our lives.

For the most part, we have not listened. But perhaps there is still time to take their message to heart and change our ways. If not, I have no doubt we will be forced to.

WERNEKE © 1990

C H A P T E R   3

The Hopi Hearings

The Hopi have thrived in the desert Southwest for hundreds of years. As one of the oldest and relatively unchanged cultures on this continent, their society is a kind of microcosm of the indigenous cultures of the planet. And that microcosm, I believe, contains a great wisdom for the modern age, if we are willing to learn from it.

Fortunately, the Hopi have always been willing to teach others. Even after Hopi children were taken away to American schools, Hopi elders and leaders repeatedly asked the federal government to send a commission to their villages—not only to listen to grievances, but to hear about the Hopi Way. On the surface, the Hopi were asking the U.S. government for a right to exist as a culturally autonomous group. They were tired of being pressured to become a part of the American melting pot. But on a deeper level, they wanted to speak directly and forcefully about their way of life and religion, in hopes that the federal government would begin to truly understand it.

For years, the federal government had ignored their request. Instead, the Hopi were asked to come to Washington, D.C., where their representatives met with officials in various departments and finally managed to arrange for a meeting at Hopiland.

In July 1955, Commissioner of Indian Affairs Glenn L. Emmons sent a special commission to Hopi to find out just what the Hopi wanted so urgently to convey to the rest of the world. The commission was composed of Assistant Commissioner Thomas M. Reid and program officers Joe Jennings and Graham Holmes. For two weeks, the Hopi in every village were allowed to air their grievances. More importantly, Hopi leaders and respected elders were able to speak publicly about the essence and importance of Hopi religion and philosophy.

The result of this conference is a little-known but remarkable document called the Hopi Hearings. Since 1955, it has been sitting on the dusty shelves of government archives, unedited and unread. I attended the hearings and afterwards obtained one of the few original copies from the Phoenix area office of the Bureau of Indian Affairs. I have kept it all these years, reading through it periodically, in hopes that there might be a time when it could be more widely circulated. I believe that time is now.

The Hopi Hearings are unique in many ways. First, they took place in an open, friendly environment conducive to a productive exchange of ideas. Such has rarely been the case in relations between Indians and government representatives in the history of the United States. Second, they contain statements by the elders of each of the Hopi villages, many of whom have since passed away.

In all, the hearings comprise more than four hundred pages of records, legends, myths, and sacred teachings—all expressed directly and informally by the Hopi themselves. Many of these testimonies help to illuminate the Hopi creation myth, as well as the myth of Pahana's return.

This document is no literary work, as its somewhat raw and rambling quality will attest. The Hopi speakers were expressing themselves in their own tongue, and their statements frequently had to be translated into English by their fellow Hopi. I include these unedited statements primarily because I believe they express the true humility, simplicity, and heart of the Hopi better than any report or anthropological study could have done. The hearings are also a unique opportunity to hear Native American religious truths expressed in their original form.

At first glance, it might be difficult to understand why the Hopi seemed so willing to publicly divulge what might be considered tribal secrets. But we should remember two things. First, Hopi culture had been misunderstood by the federal government for well over half a century. And second, the Hopi were probably more inclined to openness because their persecution by the white culture had not been as violent or as long lasting as that of most Indian tribes. Also, the Hopi really believe they are the original teachers for us all, and they freely offer their wisdom when asked.

Some observers even today might consider the Hopi's apparent trust rather naive. In fact, it was a very smart attitude for them to take. For the first time, the Hopi were able to establish in an official document the underlying reasons for their desire to be allowed to maintain their own separate culture and religion. The Hopi Hearings are, in effect, a Hopi "Declaration of Independence."

One of the most outspoken Hopi elders at the hearings was Dan Katchongva, the late Sun Clan leader of Hotevilla quoted in chapter 2. Katchongva spent more than a century on this Earth. During that time, he witnessed not only the battle between the ancient and modern worlds, but saw many Hopi prophecies fulfilled. He experienced the whole spectrum of Hopi existence, from peaceful village life to the most forceful interference the Hopi have ever known.

On the first page of the typewritten Hopi Hearings, Katchongva states the reasons for the meeting.

Yes, it is true that we had a meeting together in Washington lately and today we have come together again, and I am glad to see that you people did fulfill your promise to come and attend to this matter.

We are the first people that lived on this land. We are following our own tradition and life pattern which has been given to us and all other Indian people in this land, to follow and to live their own life in accordance with the instructions that were given to us when we first came here. All Indian people in this land receive this life plan and the instructions which they must adhere to in order that they might have a good life as long as they live on this land.

At that time we were living here alone, and there were no white people here, and all of us looking at this life and how it is a good life until a few years back the white man came to us. He came to us and our way of life was already established, and it is good to us and this is what we are still standing on.

Now when the white man came many things have happened. While the Hopi has been following this life pattern which he obtained from the Great Spirit Maasauu when he first came here. Everything seems to be working along fine, and it has been all well established and is being practiced, and the white man came along and at first it seemed the white man tried to follow the pattern of the Hopi and Indian people in this land, and they worked together and were getting along fine.

But later on it seems the white man began to bring more of his ways of life upon the Indian people, and he tries to put his plan upon us and there are many of us alarmed. This is because they are not part of our life pattern; yet we know these things will take place. And later on he began to make different rules and policies which he attempted to force upon us, and this is where we began to have trouble.

Two ways of life meeting, and one of them is trying to force his ways upon the other, and we become confused because many of us began to wonder where that will lead us. Later on we seem unable to make a step because our way of life is gradually being pushed aside . . .and we who are following and adhere to our own way of life have opposed many of these new programs of the white man, and for that reason many of us have suffered untold mistreatment because it is not our way of life and because we want to remain within our own life pattern.

On page 4 of the document, Mr. Reid recognizes an important fact:

This meeting was called by the Hopi people themselves. We are not here to conduct any directory meeting; we are here to hear the problems from you people yourselves.

Then follows a very interesting paragraph on page 6, a statement by Dan Katchongva that indicates in no uncertain terms the powerful attachment the Hopi have to their original religion. Katchongva also makes a prophetic statement about a person who will benefit from Hopi religious teachings and the sacred stone tablet originally given to the Hopi by Maasauu, guardian of the Earth.

From the time when the Oraibi people split up in 1906 in Old Oraibi, my father was taking the lead in bringing his followers to this village, he being one of the leading men, and I am the son of Acuma in trying to carry on the same duty which was placed upon him.

Today we are claiming to be the leaders. Someone is highest. Christian people tell us there is one All Mighty. There is one God, and who is that? We also know that the Hopi people obtained this sacred stone tablet which was placed in the hands of those great leaders of the Hopi people when they first came here. It was written, all these teachings, the life plan of the Hopi, and it is upon this stone tablet we base our life, and all of our religious ceremonies are connected to it.

There are many religious leaders and religious orders which carry on this life pattern and interpret all the teachings that were handed down to us by our forefathers so that we will not make a mistake of ever losing this life, but that someone—we do not know who—that person will bring these matters to a head so that we will not lose this life. That person will be benefited by this sacred stone tablet and by our religious teachings. Our religious orders are still in order and practiced. They are the lifeblood of the Hopi, and there are many people who have left that duty because of other religious teachings, but there are many religious ceremonies and rites which deal with the life pattern.

From the same village of Hotevilla, a village that claims to hold and safeguard the traditional teachings of the Hopi, another elder became very well known to a great number of white friends of the Hopi. In many ways, to these non-Hopi who were inspired to defend traditional Hopi ways at a time of assimilation, this man became the Don Quixote of the Hopi traditional cause. David Monongye, usually referred to simply as "Grandpa David," waged a lifelong fight at Hotevilla to resist modern conveniences and the concept of assimilation, which he believed would be the end of the Hopi Way.

On page 53 of the Hopi Hearings, Grandpa David gives a long and detailed exposé of the instructions given to the original Hopi by the Great Spirit. He explains why he and other traditional Hopi have so often opposed governmental plans having to do with the land—especially those that would "cut it up," as he put it. He finishes his explanation of Hopi traditional values with the following statement:

Many people are laughing at us, but this life is a very serious matter to us, and the teachings that were handed down to us are instilled in us that we must never make this mistake of losing this land and life because there is someone above watching us and is hearing us speak these words and if we ever make a mistake he will know and will punish us. That is His mission, and we must never allow ourselves to come to this end. This is the instructions that the Hopi knows will protect our life and our land. We are not to hurt or to hate anyone, but only to humble ourselves and go on with our stand and work toward that life that the Great Spirit gave us.

From the village of Hotevilla, on Third Mesa, the commissioners went to the Second Mesa village of Shungopovi. There, Andrew Hermequaftewa makes the following statement, indicating the role played by Pahana in the Hopi myth of the returning god:

The older brother was instructed to go to another part of the land and he was to go along until he reached a certain place in this land and then he would come back to look for his younger brother. This was done so that this life plan would never be destroyed

What this paragraph actually means is that the journey undertaken by the elder twin at the time of creation—a journey meant to insure a greater knowledge of the world— would guarantee that the Hopi life plan would not be destroyed. The "certain place" referred to is not necessarily a specific physical location. It may well refer to a certain time or climate of world events. The knowledge and wisdom gained by Pahana, the older questing brother, would be brought back to help the younger brother (America) and save the original life plan at a time when it was falling into chaos. This message is almost identical to those given the world by Quetzalcoatl and Christ.

Hermequaftewa then goes on speaking of the Hopi traditions given by the organizer of all life. In it, on page 87, he makes a puzzling statement about an unusual "instrument" that could be interpreted as radio, television, or even the modern computer.

Again I remind you to stand true to our tradition. They will also come to you with metal instruments of power. If the people remain true to your tradition, will not give in under the pressure or under the methods under which they want you to accept your tradition, you will always remain strong. However, if you do become weary of their persistence, of their constant approach to accept this instrument and you accept it, it will lead you to destruction.

This instrument is something that you will never be able to catch up with. It will be an instrument in which they will say yesterday that is what we said, today that doesn't hold. Every day they will change the laws. Every day additions will be made and in this method he will never catch up with it. This was told to us and this was to be the outcome if he would accept this new instrument of power and we would see our land dry up and our land would be taken away from us and even our traditional teachings would be upset.

Again he told us, do not yield to this new instrument. You boys, you young men who have no heart, they will doubtlessly bring you to this new instrument; therefore, do not make any young man ruler. Stick to your Hopi setup in selecting your rulers. Follow the Hopi initiation pattern, in which the various clans have part. As I just got through telling you, take up the initiation setup for your ruler, the Song Clan having a part, and the One Horn Clan having a part and the Two Horn Clan having a part, and the Wuchem Society having a part in this initiation. These are the clans that are to continue the leadership among your people.

On page 88 is another interesting quote: "We were instructed that we are all moving towards the day of purification, when the purifier himself will come." This is an obvious reference to the worldwide myth of the savior's return.

Again and again, the warning is sounded in the hearings about the importance of not disrupting the Hopi life plan established at the time of creation. For example, Ralph Selina has this to say on pages 98 and 99:

When we came to this life, we multiplied and covered this whole land because we were following this life pattern which we have obtained from the owner of this land and life. He must have told this thoroughly and well in establishing this life on this land for us. He has given different people their languages and way of life and their way of worshiping so that all plans of life would work out in the way he wants this life to be placed on this earth. It was a good plan, and that is why many of us even though we may be of the same people have little differences in our languages.

Let us think these problems and these instructions over very carefully. The Great Spirit has well laid down the life plan for all of us, giving each group of people their instructions and way of life and their religious beliefs so that when they go off, they would adhere to it and will obtain everlasting life.

There must be a reason for this Creator to lay down this life in this manner. He has a purpose for doing this, and if we try to disrupt this life plan, we will certainly run into trouble because we will begin to disrupt the life pattern we have received from our Great Spirit. And if each people follow their ways and beliefs and hold fast until the end, yet each in turn respect other people's way of life, I believe that this life will continue to be good and we will have everlasting life.

But it seems one group is trying to force all other people to live his way of life, thinking that it is the best way to do, but that is only working to destroy this life pattern which we have obtained from the Great Spirit. Knowing these teachings that are handed down to us and watching the white man's way of life and what he is doing, it seems that we are beginning to break up this life pattern of our Great Spirit who has laid this down for all of us.

We are looking for our white brother who is separated from us and whose duty it is to look for his brother, to find whether he is still living his way of life. This was his mission which was given to him when he first came here. And if we destroy this life in this manner when he comes and finds us disrupting our life, then he will have to punish us in some way. In order that we do not get that severe punishment, the Hopi wants to hold fast to this life pattern and to follow his religious teachings and continue to perform the duties placed upon them so that we will not destroy our own people, our land, and our life. This is the duty of the Hopi, and so we are not going to let go of this life because we are all fully aware of this white brother who will come and either destroy us or give us everlasting life.

In my time when I came to the age where I could reason things out, I knew that at that time life was good. There was plenty of crops and plenty of grass, and everything was going along fine because we were following our leaders who are doing their duty in the right manner without anyone disrupting them. Since the white man came and began to force his ways on us and trying every way with his new plans to force us into his ways, I feel that our leaders' hearts and minds are disrupted.

They began to be concerned about these things while they try to go through their ceremonies for the good of all people so that it came to a time our life began to be disrupted. And for the result we reap drought and long years of scarcity of crops, and the grass began to dry up, and I felt that these teachings that are handed down to us are true because they say that we will begin to feel the change in life if we ever become confused or doubt our way of life and begin to fall for a new life of another people.

Thinking these problems over, I feel that the proper way for us to go is to have our own leaders carry on our own life in the way they have been instructed so that we will have a good life again.

On page 105 Earl Pela sounds another warning—a warning that deals with the white brother that natives so often mistook for the long-awaited Pahana.

We have known of a prophecy that sometime our white brother would come to us, and we know his purpose was to correct any wrongs that have been done to us, and knowing this, we have always wanted to bring these out to anyone, hoping that he will be the brother we have been waiting for so that when all these things are brought out they might recognize it so they do correct some of these problems here with us. All these things were provided for us to use and to bring out to the one who comes to us, and this is the way we are looking to you people here that you might be the ones who are willing to correct some of these things and do justice to us. Land is the main thing to us because from it we obtain all our food and everything we live by, and we want to have that land to ourselves so that we will not make any mistake in this life.

On pages 124 and 125 Guy Kootshaftewa from Mishongovi gives a historical rendering of the impact made by the coming of the Spaniards to Hopiland. Here, as in many other places throughout the Hopi Hearings, it is most interesting to hear, in the Hopi's own words, evidence of the damage done to ancestral life by a dominant culture.

I want to give you a brief history and the highlights of our life. As long as our history is remembered, in the way of tradition, we are the people who at one time had another country, and the life that we left is somewhat similar to what we are living today. We had people there who were going along very good until the time comes that those very head men had been destructed by certain things that have come upon the people there at that time and in order to move on from there we have migrated to this country and met someone who already lived here and asked permission that we will live here in this country, and he is the very being that gave us a certain food that the Hopi must live by.

This is the life story that we will remember back in ancient time of our history. At the place where we have come from, at that point before the people started out, there was simply a division of these two leaders, and they were two brothers who were leading about the same number of people, and of course they said some words and instructions to one another before they started out—what are things that they will hope for—and they said to each other, "I will take this direction" and the other said to him, "I will take this direction, but we both are going in the same direction but taking different routes. If one of us gets to the destination first, there will be a certain sign of which both be well aware. By that sign we will know that one of us got to the destination first, and one of us still in a certain part of the country will be notified by that sign and will settle there and wait for his brother to return."

This brother was well instructed that he would come back and meet his brother and there they would ask one another if there was any trouble. Then, if there was, his brother would be the one who would return back to his other brother, will take simply his place in order to defend him from all this hard times along his life that he has gone through; any help that he may be asked, if he can help he will help his brother.

Any problem, anything along the life that is endurance to him and his people they will both work together and live from there on, as he said. These two brothers have taken the people around on a different route along the line of history that tells their very life and that was the instruction. First, that the sign will tell the other brother. If they see the sign they will remain there and these are the very beliefs here that were at that time the sign was seen. So they remained here in these villages and were waiting for his brother, expecting him to return at any time.

There was a duration between waiting for his brother. In the meantime, of course, the people had been expanding out, beginning to inhabit here and there and building up their villages, knowing for sure that his brother will return from there some day and will give him help. They go on and hard times occur during their life. Finally someone did come. Of course that is their expectation; someone would come to this Hopi people and there are several guesses as to whether that is the one or it may not be.

So they welcome him. He is a little different from them, but they were hoping that he is the one. As they lived on with him he began to live his ways. He began to show himself, who he was, and people began to realize of his activities, his ways of living. As they go on, he began to kind of interrupt into their religion. Finally he succeeded in persuading several people in various villages and told them that they must do away with their religion and follow his way, and the people of course began to wonder.

They said that he is very intelligent and strong in mind and strong in every way. He is now much more different as he began to reveal himself among the people, and he began to take authority upon himself. He began to rule and to dictate to the people in various villages how they should work in them. He began to practice several things that the Hopi have no knowledge of. Of course, the people who are taking his side began to take the pattern of the man, beginning to practice a lot of maliciousness among themselves, to practice several things that the Hopi himself has never thought of. These things were happening.

Finally they came to hard times because they have done away with their religion as they were forced by these people who came upon them. There was drought and no rain. There was no food for the people to live on. They decided to do something about this so they of course in these various villages began to hold meetings trying to decide on what can be done about it, in order to do away with this man after they learned that he is not their brother that they were expecting.

All began to learn that he is not the one to come and help them because he showed himself to destroy their life. So all the leaders agreed upon the date and how the punishment should take place. As history has shown, in the village of Shungopovi there is the place this punishment will take place because there is the headquarters of the people. So the people decided on a date when this will take place and the day has come and they sacrificed this man in order to revenge all of them of the punishment that have been received from these people. They burned them.

Of course, these other villages had been instructed how to do away with these other people, and on that very day they chased these other men who were with them. That is how they did away with these people, as you will recall, that is referring to the Catholics at the time when this revolution has been taking place on the Hopi.

That is the history that has been well recorded and that the people know. The people themselves were pretty well destructed in their life and in their way of supplying food. They were helpless, so they began to hold meetings again how they should figure out a way to revive their life. They began to ask one another as they held meetings.

Finally they got together and agreed that they will try, and they have decided that they will start from the beginning. In order to start the beginning of life again, they have ordained the smallest child, who has been designated to be their leader. From there on the old life started all over again and life began to regenerate and everything seemed to be beginning to grow and be plentiful.

The life began to regenerate and they realized that their religion has pretty well destructed and gone. Of course, a few things were remembered pretty well, and those things have been revived again and the life has been existing again among the Hopi from there on.

As the history goes, from there on the leaders of various villages got together and figured out that they should be aware of these things that had come upon them in the future. They should be very careful. If anyone should come upon them like it happened, any strangers that come upon them, they should not take in without questioning him. They should ask where he came from, what belief he has in himself, give him several testings before they will consider him—any way that they will think of whether to welcome him or not.

From there on these things have been pretty well instructed among the Hopi people ever since. That is why the Hopi sometimes asks many strangers of the questions that have been mentioned, to find out from the man who he is before he can have any conference with him.

Earlier, I made reference to Dan Katchongva, the late Sun Clan leader of Hotevilla. On page 260, he expresses bitterness over the realization that the white brother twice thought to have been the returning Pahana (both the Spaniards in the seventeenth century and the Americans in the nineteenth century) was in fact an invader solely interested in personal gain.

We have spoken of land and how to settle this land problem. I say no one can settle this land problem. It is going to be the one who will come who will settle this land problem. This has been warned to us, so we are still holding on to all of our life and all of our land that was designated under our stone tablet. That is when we will come to this everlasting life. That is what these stone tablets are for.

We know that one brother of ours will have the same kind of stone tablets, and we will then fully recognize each other as brothers. It is only then this land problem will be settled. We cannot settle it now. We will only make the mistake of cutting it up the white man's way.

We have been told by the white man that all livestock belonged to him. The white man has been the last one to come upon our land, yet he seems to know everything about Hopi people or Indian people. That is what he claims. If he did, these problems would not have come up in this way. You have claimed everything: our land, our forests, our wild game. And you want to make us pay for these things. This is not the way a person should do.

Now we have to be paying for those things that were ours in former times. If you know us, you would have followed up our ruins where we have lived, and you would have come to us and known us, but instead you have come claiming everything for yourselves. Now the question was brought before you at one of our meetings whether this land belonged to the Hopi or the white man, and you said the government is not the one trying to take the land away from the Hopi, but only the Navajos.

Indeed, the Hopi Hearings give us a unique opportunity to measure the damage done to a pristine native society by a more sophisticated, technological society. Today, it is very difficult to find records of myths, legends, and teachings bequeathed solely through oral tradition.

Though it is not possible or even desirable to quote more than a few of these oral texts, I believe some passages are essential to an understanding of what this book is all about. One of these is the recollection of John Lomavaya—a sacred oral teaching he probably heard during gatherings of elders in his village kiva. More than any other section of the Hopi Hearings, this one reveals the nature of the original twins' mission in the Hopi myth of creation.

My story relates to tradition that is versed in the leaders, we call them. The things that I would state myself are the traditions of the Snake Clan. I have gone along in life and met up with life in a different form and shape. The light has been shone in my path whereby I am trying to live according to the light that has been shown me, and that is where I am standing by giving you the information. [Interpreter: meaning he is a Christian by faith.]

The tradition that I am going to relate to you refers back to the dim past where humanity first existed down below. It was populated with people, and they have reached the point where darkness shadowed them, and it starts with two brothers who are involved.

I mentioned that it involves two brothers, the elder and the younger brother. The elder brother told the young brother that they must separate and go their way. The elder brother said, "I intend to go on the right hand, on the right side of the path. I intend to go on this journey not laden with a lot of burdens. I aim to seek where there is true, clean life, if I can reach my destiny. I am going to make this trip eastward, and if I can reach the point where I will be able to touch my forehead and gain what I am after, I will make my retreat and return. I am after things that are good and necessary."

Then the younger brother spoke. "So that is what you are going to do. I will take the left-hand path and I will travel with many things and have many burdens. It will take some time before I can reach my destination. I will take my time and amuse myself as I go along, and I will not be hurrying along. But if you should reach your destiny, as you say, seeking the right things in life, after you make your retreat, we will meet again somewhere while I am on my way to my destiny. When you meet me, I will live the life that you might bring to me."

The younger brother continued, "When you start out, should you reach your destination, by what sign would you give me when you make your retreat?"

The elder brother responded, "When I make my retreat, I will give you a sign by having certain stars fall, and when you see this sign, you will want to prepare to start to get rid of things that are burdening you so that when I meet you, you will have your burdens in a light manner."

So spoke the older brother. These are the things that they have spoken to one another as brothers. There were many people down there, and each brother was to go his way, and also the people that were down there. There were many languages spoken by these people. The place where they emerged from is very vague. I cannot state just how they came upon this land, but, nevertheless, they came upon this land. So there they started out, each one paying heed for signs that might appear.

Speaking of his brother, he meant a person with a white skin whom he called his elder brother. I have said that there were many languages spoken when they came on this earth. The one who was recognized as their leader called them together. The leader placed ten ears of corn on the ground. One was a perfect ear, that was placed at the extreme end when the corn was placed, and with this instruction that he gave to the people, and he said, "Now should we be met by our brother in the future, anybody that takes this perfect ear of corn will have to meet up with whatever circumstances he might have to consider."

These were the instructions he gave to the people. After the people heard what the leader said, they of course stood around not knowing what to do. They hesitated for quite a lengthy time until afterwards there was a certain man, or one who represented that certain group, by the name of Yo-ta-hani. In other words, what the Spanish have given the name of "Navajo."

He stood up and walked over to the line of corn that was on the ground. He looked at the congregation there and said, "If you people do not desire to take this up, let it be me. I will enjoy everything that is to come: wealth, stock, and even the fair maidens that might be involved."

When this Yo-ta-hani, the Navajo, picked the corn up, the leader looked at him not approvingly and made this remark: "Because that perfect ear meant something in life that is perfect and good, but he made his own statement that he would have access to wealth, stock and women, is why the leader looked at him in that manner. I do not approve of that Navajo because he is an aggressive individual. He wants to get the best and the first things, and then if he is even down flat on his back he still can resist and fight and kick."

Afterwards, others walked up and picked up these ears for themselves. Lastly the Hopi. He was the last person to walk up there and what was left was just a short ear. That ear the Hopi picked up for himself.

After this took place, each group that spoke the same language went their way in groups, because many languages were spoken. From there on, those who were known as Hopi started out on their journey, and before he moved to the next place he always made a practice of looking to the direction where his brother went to before he moved on.

Of course, it has been said that Hopi has covered a big territory. He went all over the country, and wherever he went he still looked towards where his brother went and for certain signs that were to be given. In going about over the country, he left countries that are rich, countries that are running with water, until whenever he meets up with someone that is not what he wants to find, he usually puts it aside and goes on.

Every time he moves, he still looks for and seeks to see if there is a sign. He kept on going. He made his journey climbing to higher land and when he came up on this high plateau, he found that there was nothing here. It was barren. The only thing that moistens the land was drizzling rain. That is what he depended upon, because he don't want to have land taken away from him in the future.

The Hopi must have covered a big territory in his wanderings, because of the evidence of ruins that he has left in his roaming. Finally he arrived in this country, and the place that was designated as his last residence was Navajo Mountain.[4]

It is impossible not to be struck by the many warnings contained in the Hopi elders' statements—warnings that stand like lampposts marking the path of human behavior. As we will see in subsequent chapters, such warnings are not unique to the Hopi culture. They are present in the age-old traditions of cultures all around the world.

But as far as the Hopi are concerned, the four hundred pages of typewritten material that make up the Hopi Hearings are consistent in their main messages. First, the Hopi believe they are the repository of the initial instructions given to humankind by its maker. Secondly, they believe that at least some of their ancestors originally came from "another country"—a country, as I will later show, that most likely is part of Central America.

Because of their ancient history, I believe the Hopi are, in their ceremonial and religious endeavors, the repository of extremely ancient rituals. If this is true, then the Hopi can quite legitimately claim that their religious and cultural survival is of great importance to the world at large.

This and other Hopi claims and prophecies are often difficult for a huge and powerful society like ours to accept. On what authority, we might ask, do the economically and militarily insignificant Hopi pretend to offer prophecy for the future of the world? Yet in asking such questions, we confuse might with wisdom and forget the power in simplicity.

As one who has lived with the Hopi, I can say from firsthand experience that their messages flow not from arrogance but from a deep reverence and humility. We do not have to take the Hopi at their word, but we had better listen to them and take a good look at what is happening in the world. After an honest appraisal, I believe even the most seasoned skeptic would be alarmed at how much truth they have told.

C H A P T E R 4

Old World Myths of the Supernatural Return

I would like to begin this chapter with a short exploration of the nature of myth. In his *Primitive Psychology*, published in London in 1926, Bronislaw Malinowski gives the following definition of myth:

> Myth is an established link between the past and the present. As it exists in its living primitive form, it is not merely a story told, but a reality lived. It is not of the nature of fiction, such as we read today in a novel, but it is a living reality, believed to have once happened in primeval times, and continuing ever since to influence the world and human destinies . . .
>
> These stories live not by idle interest, not as fictitious or even as true narratives, but are to the natives a statement of a primeval, greater, and more relevant reality, by which the present life, fates, and activities of mankind are determined, the knowledge of which supplies man with the motive for ritual and moral actions, as well as with indications as to how to perform them.[5]

Regarding Malinowski's statement, it is pertinent to state that myth generally relates an important event usually attributed to a godly figure, a hero, or even an ordinary mortal. But this event is always destined to have never-ending consequences.

Professor Peter Grimal of the Sorbonne University in Paris adds:

> There are also more subtle myths, which report a renewable creative act and make it possible, by means of rites, to commence a part of creation all over again in present time.

This statement in particular serves well the concept of the myth of the returning god as it became incorporated in the mythic past of both the ancient and the new world.

It also should be pointed out that myth is not an intellectual manifestation of either individual or collective consciousness, but an instinctive choice accepted by all the beings in a given society. It is more a product of faith than of reasoning. In believing in the myth, one becomes a part of it, lives it as it unfolds in the present.

In other words, for both an individual and a group, believing in a myth makes it a historical fact. In a very real way, then, myths effect changes that make history. This is important to realize, as we are about to connect the myth of the supernatural divine return to historical reality.

One striking modern example of the synchronicity of myth and history was Harmonic Convergence of 1987. That summer, tens of thousands of people all around the planet gathered in a ritual expression of their faith that the planet had just entered a new age. This was the beginning of a myth based on world collective consciousness, the inner desire for a planetary spiritual initiation.

Most interestingly, Harmonic Convergence was predicted by many ancient societies, including the Maya, Incas, and Aztecs. And, indeed, this worldwide ritual appeared to be a kind of spiritual opening, the lifting of the curtain on a planetary symphony highlighting a world in transformation.

Exactly what will come of Harmonic Convergence remains to be seen. It is the beginning of a dream that is not yet finished. But I think it is safe to say that this event, like all mythical events, will profoundly affect the future of a large population. As Peter Grimal would say, "Myths do not die. . . . They become tomorrow's reality. In them are the secret teachings of the past. They are the spiritual prehistory of a society."

Now comes the big question: Are the Indo-European myths of creation similar and possibly even identical to those of Mesoamerica? For the answer, we must look to the study of world mythology.

The elements of creation myths that would encompass all the world civilizations can be found in the mythologies of ancient Sumeria, Chaldea, Babylon, the Hittite world, Persia, Egypt, Greece, and Rome, as well as in the present world of Christianity. In other words, it seems that from the Indus-Tigris-Euphrates region, now called the Middle East, comes the substance of a myth of creation that is extremely similar to the myths of creation that come from Mesoamerica, as I will illustrate.

The white, bearded teacher of Mesoamerican myths and legends has several names: Kukulcan, Quetzalcoatl, and Pahana. This is essentially the same personality whose passage is recorded by most Native American cultures. Though details differ in various cultures, the message this mythical personality left behind is essentially the same as that left by those in myths and legends of the Middle East.

Sumeria: 3200-2100 B.C.

Sumeria was located in the present geographical area of Syria, Iraq, and Iran. This ancient kingdom is believed to have given rise to the Indo-European world, from which modern-day Europe arose. Part of what is now Turkey was also included in the Sumerian kingdom. It is there, on Mount Ararat, that Noah's Ark is believed to have landed when the flood finally receded.

The cosmological myth of origin in Sumeria is found in a work called "The Poem of Creation." This is an account of the work of the gods in primeval times when Earth and sky were called "the twins." It is of special interest to note that the myths of the various societies that arose from Sumeria, such as the Enuma Elish (the Babylonian flood epic), are the core of the essential creation stories that were later recounted in the Old Testament of the Bible. The Egyptians had similar creation myths, and the Greeks expressed their versions of the Sumerian myths in theatrical tragedies that eventually became the pillars of what is now Western consciousness.

In short, the same script has been written time and time again. By the time Jesus was born, he had only to play the part in such an impeccable way that his life became a part of humanity's continuing lifeline of story.

Babylon: 2100-1595 B.C.

Babylonian myths gradually followed the ancient Sumerian myths, and many scholars concur that Babylonian myths are adaptations of earlier Sumerian myths that were rediscovered by Western archaeologists only in the twentieth century.

In Babylonian mythology we find an adaptation of "The Poem of

Creation" that includes a very provocative section—a section that confirms that the original myth is being passed from one civilization to the next. It is fascinating to note that we can speculate that the Christian doctrine of redemption of mankind by the blood of Christ can be traced to the so-called pagan pre-Christian world several thousand years earlier.

As the *Larousse World Mythology* puts it on page 67, "The reply to Ea [the Babylonian main god] returns to one of the favorite themes of Mesopotamian theology: that is the creation of mankind from the blood of a god who had been sacrificed, a theme that will be found again and again in numerous independent myths in the Poem of Creation."

As we will see when analyzing some of the Egyptian myths, especially that of Isis and Osiris, a new dimension to the myth is added, namely, that of the resurrection of the god that has been sacrificed. As we continue studying the "Poem of Creation" from the Babylonian period, we find that another major god, Marduk, symbolizes both the cosmic order and the sun. In his capacity as a sun god, Marduk also symbolizes the forces of spring that are now incorporated into the Christian calendar as Easter.

The victory of spring (life) over the forces of winter (death) was one of the hard-held tenets of the Babylonians, who celebrated the spring equinox as the rebirth of the year, sanctifying the continuity of the ordered world.

Two of the stanzas in the Babylonian "Poem of Creation," called the "Cosmology of Assur," are particularly interesting for our purposes. These stanzas take up the theme of the sacrificed god, expressing the creation of Earth and sky and the birth of humanity in the following way:

> When the Sky had been separated from the Earth,
> Constant and remote twins,
> When the mother of the gods had been created,
> When the Earth had been created and fashioned
> And the destinies of the Sky and the Earth fixed. . .
> Out of his blood they fashioned mankind,
> He imposed the service and let free the gods.
> After Ea, the wise, had created mankind,

> He imposed upon it the service of the gods—
> That working beyond comprehension:
> As artfully planned by Marduk
> Did Nudimmud create it.

Related thoughts are expressed in the Hopi "Song of Creation," which deals with the Hopi migrations and humanity's ultimate dependence on cosmic forces:

> From the four corners of the universe:
> > From the East, for red is its color;
> > From the North, for white is its color;
> > From the West, for yellow is its color;
> > And from the South, for black is its color;
> In the counterclockwise motion of *Tawa Taka*,
> > the Sun Father,
> Come the four colors of the races of humankind,
> > each with its leaders,
> > each with its destiny.
> Soon they will fight, as it is prophesied,
> but someday they shall unite.
> > Then they will remember
> > that Taiowa is their spirit father;
> > that Sotuknang is their adoptive one;
> > and that Spider Woman is the web
> > which unites them all.

Persia: 538-331 B.C.

In the myths of Persia (present-day Iran), we discover that the idea of the world appearing out of ritual sacrifice leads to a transformation of mythical elements into the dualism of good and evil called Mazdaism.

The great mythical personality of that period was Zarathustra, a divine human who could be compared to the feathered serpent Quetzalcoatl of Mesoamerica. In some ways, Zarathustra added a new dimension to the notion of the godly sacrifice bringing a renewal of the universe. First, his sacrifice was bound to the cycle of the seasons. And second, it was bound to the doctrine of salvation. This is the same concept as the Second Coming of Christ or the Pahana of the Hopi returning to help salvage the world from certain chaos and collapse.

Moreover, Zarathustra is thought to be related to two figures, or twins: initial and final, primeval man and the ultimate savior. He transcends his human historical role as king and emperor to become a character of cosmic proportions, much like Quetzalcoatl in the Americas.

It is easy to see, then, that the Christian concept of the resurrection of the body on Judgment Day can be traced to the Persian myth that took its cyclic structure from a ritual called Haoma, prototype of the ultimate recreative sacrifice that gives back life and reestablishes creation in its original state.

The belief in individual reincarnation also could be an extension of the belief in the global resurrection of the Last Judgment. Rather than a sudden planetary awakening, "resurrection" is carried out in stages, one individual at a time.

To sum up what has to be learned from the concepts of the progression of these sacrificial personalities, it is vital to mention the myths of ancient Egypt as well.

With Egyptian mythology, we find classic solar mythology. Along with all major cultures of antiquity, the solar calendar was a projection of the daily cycle of the sun—its daily birth at sunrise and its daily death at dusk. Gradually, though, this daily cycle is expanded into much larger cycles—cycles of a thousand years involving the birth and death of the world and even longer cycles involving the birth, rise, and decline of civilizations.

The principal religious cults that shaped Egyptian culture were Re, the sun god; Osiris, the god of death and resurrection; and Isis, the goddess who rescues Osiris from the dead. The sun is an omnipresent force in Egypt, as it rises almost every day in a hot, cloudless sky. It is easy to understand why the Egyptians adored the sun as the giver of life and saw in its progress the pattern of life perpetually renewed. Every night Re died in the west and every morning he was reborn in the east.[6]

The cult of Osiris includes Isis, his wife and sister, and their son, Horus. At one time, Osiris must have been a wise and humane earthly ruler, for he persuaded the Egyptians to give up cannibalism and introduced them to the making of arts and crafts. But eventually he was elevated to the status of an already-existing god, becoming a kind of Quetzalcoatl of the Near East.

Osiris also had a brother named Seth. According to the myth, Seth was insanely jealous of his brother and managed to kill Osiris. Afterwards, he cut his body into small pieces, burying them in various parts of Egypt—all except the penis, which he threw into the River Nile.

Isis recovered all the parts of her husband's body except the penis, which had been washed away. She reassembled the parts and reanimated the corpse. Without his reproductive organ, Osiris could no longer be a king of mortals. Instead he became a god—the god of the dead and the judge of souls.

This myth might have entered the collective consciousness of the Egyptian culture because of an earlier custom in which the king (also called a pharaoh) was sacrificed after reigning a certain number of years and was then considered a god.

Two thoughts come to mind to explain the similarity of Indo-European and Mesoamerican myths. One is that the Old World myths could have been brought into the New World by early groups of seafaring explorers and settlers. Another is that the thought processes of the human brain—the great movements of the collective subconscious—could have produced similar myths in different parts of the world. Whatever happened, it is remarkable that from 4000 B.C. to A.D. 800 or so, almost identical myths were embraced by extremely different peoples all over the world.

Here, of course, we have been talking about legends and myths recollected over a period of from four to six thousand years. But what about before that? How far back do the myths go? Are some of the early schools of thought influenced by explorers from other galaxies, as the prophesies of Ezekiel and some Sumerian texts would have us believe? No one can say with certainty, but the similarities in myths of all cultures attest to their meaning and importance for ancient and modern people alike.

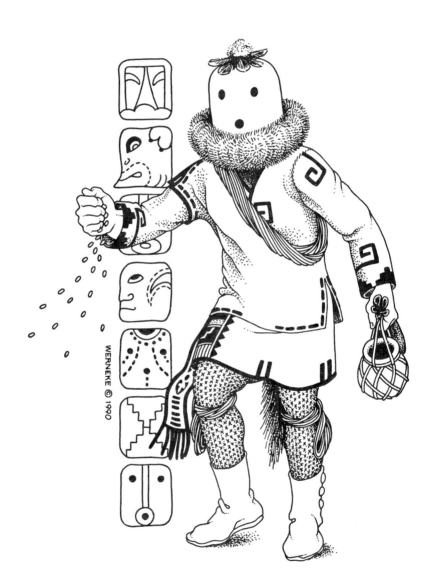

WERNEKE © 1990

New World Myths of the Supernatural Return

Looking at the creation myths of the Native American cultures, we find definite similarities between those of the Hopi, Aztecs, Maya, Incas, and others. The most striking similarity concerns the appearance of "twins," or an elder brother or godly figure who sacrifices himself as a purification for his people, and who serves as both witness and judge to confront humanity with its pledge to follow the path the Creator has originally established for it.

The *Popol Vuh*, or *Book of Advice*, an ancient Mayan manuscript, speaks of a legendary cycle involving twins who are identified as two real deities, two brothers called Hunahpu and Xbalanque. After slaying a number of terrible giants, these two have countless adventures together:

> They seem like demiurges whose acts affected the world. Their sphere of activity covered both the world of Earth and the world below (in Hopi mythology, Maasauu holds the same authority). They were the creators of "magic," their acts being repeated in the echoing gestures of the sorcerer by the process known as "sympathy."[7]

The ultimate sources to consult on the roles played by the twins in Mayan theology are two of the original texts that survived the Spanish invasions: the *Popol Vuh*, which was compiled in the Quiche dialect, and the *Chilam Balam*, which is a collection of chronicles dealing with the prophecies and history of the Yucatán.

As in so many other ancient societies, the sun played a central role in Mayan beliefs, ceremonies, and rituals. "Ahau Kines" was the Mayan term for "Lords of the Sun," and it was under their constant influence that the Maya practiced their religion of the sun, known as the great

"planetary solar cult." It was through communication with the Ahau
Kines that the great teachers like Buddha, Christ, and Quezalcoatl kept
the evolutionary memory alive.

Not unexpectedly, there are differences between the Mayan myth
of Quetzalcoatl (whom they call Kukulcan) and the Aztecs' strikingly
similar myth in Nahuatl. In the Mayan version, the twin gods, Quetzalcoatl and Tezcatlipoca, descend into the underworld, where they
throw themselves into the fire and are transformed into the sun and
the moon.

In the Puebloan community of Zuni, in New Mexico, the twins
are called the Twin Brothers of Light, or the Elder and the Younger, or
the Right and the Left. They are said to have been "born after the Sun
Father impregnated a foam cap on the Great Waters, near the Earth
Mother."[8]

The Hopi myth of the creation is very similar to that of the Maya.
In this story, Spider Woman took some earth and spat on it and then
molded it into the first two beings.[9] The Hopi names for these two are
Pokanghoya and Palongawhoya. Pokanghoya was the one on the right,
and he was ordered to go all the way around the world to solidify the
Earth. Palongawhoya, on the left, was ordered to encirle the world
while sending out sound.

There is plenty of evidence to sustain the concept of a Hopi-
Mayan connection. Part of the evidence is that two of the main Hopi
kachinas, called the "fathers of all kachinas," are believed to have come
from Mayan territory during the Hopi migrations. The names of these
kachinas are Aholi and Eototo.

In addition, one of the Mayan solar lords, Ahau, has a hieroglyphic symbol that is identical to that of a Hopi ceremonial kachina
mask. Other Mayan supernatural beings, including Akbal, Chuen, Eb,
Ix, Etznab, and Oc also have hieroglyphic symbols represented on
today's Hopi masks.

There is other evidence for the Hopi-Mayan connection as well.
One of the strongest indications is that the Hopi tongue has a Uto-
Aztecan root similar to that of the Nahuatl-speaking people of Mexico. Moreover, I have been trying for years to find out why Hopi kivas
are rectangular instead of circular, as in most of the other pueblos and
pueblo ruins of the Southwest. Not long ago, a Hopi elder noted that

the temples on top of Central American pyramids are also either square or rectangular. And finally, I recently visited Mexico myself and came away convinced that the "Red City of the South" referred to in Hopi myth is none other than the sacred Mayan city of Palenque.

The Central and South American connection, and especially the myth of the twins, is an essential root of the native mythology of the North American continent. It has been mentioned by many students of American history. Among them is photographer-anthropologist Edward S. Curtis, who includes it in *The Hopi*, the twelfth volume of his famous twenty-volume series, The North American Indian (Norwood, MA: Plimpton Press, 1922). Frank Waters also holds a prominent place as a chronicler of Mesoamerican history, and he, too, writes extensively about the myth in a number of works, including *Book of the Hopi*, *Mexico Mystique*, and *Masked Gods*. It is covered as well in William H. Prescott's *History of the Conquest of Mexico* and *History of the Conquest of Peru*, in José Argüelles's *The Mayan Factor*, in Larry Tyler's *Mayan Cycleology*, and in Loren McIntyre's *The Incredible Incas and Their Timeless Land*.

Finally, I must mention a very special study made by L. Taylor Hansen, published under the title of *He Walked the Americas*. Hansen, who holds master's degrees in archaeology, anthropology, and geology, studied the Indian societies of the Americas for thirty years. She also did research in North Africa as a recognized expert in Egyptology. As such, she was most qualified to collect stories directly from elders and native groups—stories about a legendary Caucasian bearded teacher whose presence had been remembered by a large number of Native American groups from Alaska to Tierra del Fuego.

Reading the stories Hansen collected is an unforgettable experience. The wanderings of this white teacher take the reader all over Native America. The text of the back cover gives a comprehensive summary of *He Walked the Americas*, so that more people will be made aware of this important work:

> Almost 2,000 years ago, a mysterious white man walked
> from tribe to tribe among the American nations. He came to
> Peru from the Pacific. He travelled through South and Central
> America among the Maya, into Mexico and all of North
> America, then back to ancient Tula, from where he departed

across the Atlantic to the land of his origin. Who was this white prophet who spoke a thousand languages, healed the sick, raised the dead and taught in the manner Jesus Himself did?[10]

As reported by Hansen, the bearded-teacher legend—probably part myth and part history—is very similar to the Quetzalcoatl myth. Quezalcoatl is also reported to have been a fair-skinned, bearded teacher, part emperor and part holy man. The authenticity of the personality of Quetzalcoatl is supported by a large body of literary works. Regardless of differences in interpretation, his personality as described by various sources retains a remarkable constancy. From this body of literature, it is possible to draw the following conclusions:

First, the bearded man preaching a gospel of humanity and love might have been embodied by not one but several men, possibly priests of the cult of Quetzalcoatl. Second, it is said that one of these "Quetzalcoatls" was ostracized and banished because of his teachings of love and compassion. When deported, he left in a northeasterly direction toward the waters of the Atlantic Ocean, promising to return to serve the people he loved in time of need.

After the invasions of Hernando Cortez and Francisco Pizarro into Central and South America, it is probable that the original native myths were tainted by Christian beliefs. Many indigenous people of Mesoamerica are disturbed by the description of Quetzalcoatl as a "white man," since the source of this story may be a result of Christianity. However, it is not difficult to see why certain native groups believed that Jesus Christ was the reincarnation of Quetzalcoatl.

This theory has been advanced by many scholars. It is a theory with scope enough to encompass not only the mission of Quetzalcoatl, but that of Pahana and even Jesus Christ. Whatever the source, the myths of a return of a being from an alien source indicate a great urge for the return of a god, a teacher, to uplift humanity.

Could it be that the time of the return is now? Could it be that the return, awaited by so many cultures for so long, will not take the devastating form it took with Cortez, Pizarro, or the Pilgrims, but, at last, the form of the true teacher longing to come back home?

As we can see, the myths of the Hopi Pahana and the Mesoamerican myth of Quetzalcoatl are essentially one and the same, as are many other myths from other times and places. As modern observers, then, we are confronted with basically the same myth appearing at different times on different parts of the planet. The differences in interpretation spring not so much from basic differences in the myths themselves as from cultural, geographic, and historical factors.

Given this fact, it seems logical to conclude that a large part of humanity is awaiting a monumental event—an event that, however it may manifest in the mythology of a given culture, springs from a single source. That event is the prophesied return of the missing brother, the return of peace, harmony, and spiritual light to a world fast slipping into chaos.

In the following chapter, we will take a closer look at this planetary myth in relation to modern society. But before we close this chapter, I would like to share the following lines, borrowed from the book *The Story of Quetzalcoatl*, by poet-scholar Jim Berenholtz:

THE RETURN OF QUETZALCOATL

Quetzalcoatl. Quetzalcoatl.
Being that lives where the silent seas of yesterday's rain
are washing on the empty shores of time.
At last, we witness the cracking.
From within the Void, the Conch resounds again.

KNOW that all who live in his magnified Presence
are forever advancing towards the moment of Great
    Realization
in their lives.
The Light that shines in the Silence,
in that space of Awakening,
is beyond the brilliance of even the greatest Sun.
It is the Light of your Heart,
and your Heart is the Morning Star.
O listen if you would,
for therein lies a teaching.

Joy is a gift from Universe and Divinity.
Sorrow and Pain are there for the healing.
Through touching of the Heart, the Heart is Opened.
then the Knowledge may enter,
to return the seeker to Balance.

Watch now, for the Joy and Sorrow dance Together,
and in that is their dissolution,
leaving nothing to perceive but Truth.
Embrace the Truth, for always it is precisely who you are
in your Eternal Being.
All is You.
And surrounding this all is the infinite embrace of the
    Brilliant One,
Quetzalcoatl.
Praised be his presence forever in All our Worlds.

WERNEKE ©1990

CHAPTER 6

The Myth &
the Contemporary Scene

Today's world is no longer a puzzle made up of large and small nations with little or no interaction. Because of telecommunications and modern transportation, we are now living in a global village—a village in which all nations are intimately interconnected.

Along with this shrinking of the globe, Earth's inhabitants are feeling increased apprehension, in part from the tensions of living in a fish bowl. Subconsciously at least, we are more than a little upset and frightened over the prospect of planetary interdependency.

One manifestation of this fright is that many of us suddenly feel we are running out of time. We do not have the hours to follow up on all the choices presented to us. In order to adapt to the changes and opportunities so lavishly offered in the last hundred years—in order to keep our sanity, really—we must first develop a basic understanding of the situation. The first step toward understanding is that there have been more changes in the last hundred years than in the preceding ten thousand. In spite of our veneer of sophistication, we are still primal beings naturally adapted to life in a much simpler environment. For this reason, it might be useful to study the lives of native peoples, many of whose societies, I believe, can help put us back onto the road to sanity.

One major difference between the native world and the so-called "civilized" world is that the native mind sees creation as an ongoing process rather than the result of a single act, such as the "Big Bang" that scientists believe set the universe in motion. The main consequence of this point of view is that the native world adapts to widespread changes much more readily than modern society does. Basically, native society feels comfortable with change, relying on its myths and ceremonies to carry it through. Modern society, on the other hand, feels confused and lost.

Such is the situation at the beginning of the greatest change the planet has known in thousands of years—a change that was heralded in August 1987 by Harmonic Convergence. What made this event so special? And how can we understand it on a conscious, logical level when it speaks more directly to the subconscious and spiritual—the level Teilhard de Chardin referred to as the "noosphere"?

It has been said of Harmonic Convergence that it signifies the moment when present-day industrial civilization first begins to synchronize with the natural processes of the planet. When the time is right for structural transformations to take place, they happen automatically.

According to José Argüelles, whose book *The Mayan Factor* links Harmonic Convergence with ancient Mayan prophecies, the structure of the world and human consciousness are destined for massive changes over a period of twenty-five years dating from the moment of Harmonic Convergence. Many other sources also point to such a transformation, including Tibetan and East Indian prophecies, Hopi prophecies, and even the Bible in its prediction of a "new heaven and a new earth" in Revelation 21:1-2.

The work of scholars such as Peter Russell (author of *The Global Brain*) and Rupert Sheldrake (an expert on morphogenetic fields) would suggest that Harmonic Convergence and its global consequences are the result of the "hundredth monkey" phenomenon—the idea that resonance is the determining factor in how we think about and create our experience in the world. Simply put, it suggests that all people react to each other's thoughts and that humanity as a whole experiences major growth or change when the number of humans of like mind reaches a "critical mass."

If it is true that our common memory patterns and beliefs shape the world as we know it, then the way to change the world is to create a new memory field. The key to changing the resonance is a "trigger event" such as Harmonic Convergence, in which 144,000 humans are linked together at a specific moment. This, so the theory goes, creates a minimum human voltage to cause a leap of the imagination for a critical mass of humanity, thus establishing the infrastructure of a new world order.

This phenomenon is not as far fetched as it might seem. History abounds with relatively small morphogenetic changes that altered the perceptions and actions of millions of people almost instantaneously. One such new world order was the sudden establishment of the Communist Bolshevik philosophy after the Russian Revolution of 1917. Harmonic Convergence heralds a similar but much more widespread change.

The first phase of the "trigger event" for Harmonic Convergence took place from May 4 through May 6, 1987, at the sacred site of Machu Picchu, Peru. According to modern seers, Machu Picchu is the hub of a great wheel around which revolve twelve other key sacred sites. Representatives at all these sites prayed and meditated for three days, initiating a mystical climate that helped introduce Harmonic Convergence to the world. Together, they created a vortex of energy conducive to the initiation of a new morphogenetic field. This passage from one field to another signaled a phase shift, a collective determination to shed the old world view of competitive conflict and dependence on technology and to view the world from a perspective of collaborative cooperation. Thus Harmonic Convergence may well be a cosmic "overture," the lifting of the curtain on a fantastic planetary symphony.

Members of the traditional native world are well aware of the significance of Harmonic Convergence. Their myths have prepared them for it. In accordance with those myths, those beacons of life that have guided countless tribes since time immemorial, they are preparing themselves for a new and much happier phase of collective human behavior.

It is interesting to note that alongside the transformations mentioned above, a paradoxically new and ancient trend surfaced in the belief systems of modern society. This trend began in the sixties, when New Age beliefs first began to influence the thought processes of the day, when gurus and yogis began importing spiritual outlooks and techniques from the East. As meditation and yogic techniques spread in the West, many young and not-so-young people found themselves attracted to ancient pagan rituals: Druidic, shamanic, Native American. Tibetan lamas and rinpoches also contributed to the West's new hunger for ancient religious practices.

The fact is that Judeo-Christian traditions no longer satisfy the spiritual needs of many Westerners. This, too, is indicative of the broad changes that have affected the world in recent years. Thus, Harmonic Convergence and the spontaneous initiation of a new world order responds to a deep spiritual hunger in the West—a hunger brought about by the emptiness of the values spawned by a world out of balance.

Is this return to ancient ways a sign that the return of Pahana is near? It is significant that a definite revival of ceremonial and ritualistic life has taken place in recent years among the Hopi and many Native American groups.

On the other hand, we do not need to focus on the esoteric to find evidence of planetary revolution. Many more obvious signs indicate that change is already well under way. Among them are overpopulation, famine, AIDS, drug consumption, and crime, not to mention the catastrophic destruction of the world environment itself. We are also much more frantic than our forefathers were in centuries past. In this push-button age, we crowd in a great deal more activity than ever before. In so doing, we stress our minds and bodies to the breaking point, and, ironically, we run out of time. It is clear that humankind is losing control of its destiny.

However, the scene is not altogether bleak. In fact, some planetary miracles are also occurring—for example, the democratization of the Soviet Bloc countries and the waning specter of nuclear confrontation. But regardless of the events of the near future, there is no getting around the fact that the world of 2020 will be vastly different from the world of today.

Does all this change herald the return of Christ, or Quetzalcoatl, or Pahana? Probably so. At the very least, I believe it is fair to say that humanity has entered a period in which the individual comes to grips with his or her own power.

In my view, political, economic, financial, and religious institutions are only a projection of the mind. The collective body of humanity is only the stage on which the real actor, the individual, performs between the revolving doors of birth and death. It can also be said, I believe, that the individual entries and exits of actors on this stage are part of a much longer performance—a performance that will go on until the grand finale brings everyone together for the final bow and the celebration of a performance well done.

Of course, it might be premature to assume that now is the time for the return of Christ or Pahana. After all, both humanity and the Earth have been in a state of transformation since the beginning ot time. But anyone who takes an honest look at society's problems, I think, would have to conclude that we are due for a change—and quite a drastic change, at that.

CHAPTER 7

Is Humanity Ready for a Second Coming?

When Jesus was asked by his disciples when they would see signs of his return, he answered them, "A generation will not pass before this world comes to an end."

With this admonition, it seems that the Second Coming began almost immediately and has been happening gradually for almost two thousand years—either that or the translation of the word "generation" from Aramean to Greek and then to Latin and finally into English created some confusion about Jesus' true meaning. It is possible Jesus might have been speaking about a cycle of two thousand years, which in other terms could be taken as an era or a generation in a broader spiritual context such as that used by the Maya.

If the Second Coming is at hand, how can we recognize it and prepare ourselves for it? And, ultimately, how should we respond to it?

First of all, in what form might we expect to recognize this "savior," "helper," or "brother"? In the Jerusalem Bible, the apostle John tells us to look for the coming of the "advocate." In John 16:7-8, he quotes Jesus as follows:

> The advocate will not come to you,
> But if I do go,
> I will send him to you.
> And when he comes,
> He will show the world how wrong it was.

Then there is this passage from Matthew 24:3:

> The coming of the Son of Man will be evident
> Because the coming of the Son of Man will be like
>   lightning

Striking in the East and flashing far into
    the West.
Immediately after the distress of those days,
    the Sun will be darkened,
The Moon will lose its brightness,
The stars will fall from the sky,
And then the sign of the Son of Man will appear
    in the heavens.

What will this sign across the sky be like? In 21:4, Luke says (under "Cosmic Disasters and the Coming of the Son of Man"), "On Earth, nations will be in agony and men will be dying of fear as they await what menaces the world."

Later on, in Luke 21:29-36, Luke goes on to say, "Be on the alert . . . that day will be sprung on you suddenly like a trap . . . . Stay awake, praying at all times for the strength to survive all that is going to happen, and to stand in confidence before the Son of Man."

Several of these signs have already manifested. For example, the emissions of carbon dioxide and other pollutants that have affected the Earth's atmosphere have definitely decreased the brightness of the sun and moon in some parts of the world.

Let us look at evidence of the Second Coming in the visions of Native Americans. In some ways, this is more difficult because many Mayan, Aztec, and Incan records of prophecy were obliterated by the invading Spaniards. Some of these predictions were recorded either on maguey paper, called "codices," or painted in frescoes of rare beauty on the walls of sacred temples and pyramid chambers. Others were magnificently carved on slabs of stone called stelae. Unfortunately, history is full of situations in which an invading civilization imposes its own religion after the destruction of the records of the vanquished. As far as Quetzalcoatl is concerned, then, we will have to rely mainly on oral tradition.

Chances are, neither Quetzalcoatl nor Pahana will return as a single individual, but as a group of individuals collectively bearing the characteristics of these mythical saviors. The message of these groups will be of unmistakable clarity and compassion. As the apostle Matthew says in Matthew 24:3, "The coming of the Son of Man will be evident." That is, it might manifest itself as a condition, a teaching, a new dimension of thought, or a number of events that will carry the overall message.

One clue is that in the days of the Toltec and Aztec civilizations, the political and religious leaders who attained the highest level of spiritual evolution were given the title of "Quetzalcoatl," signifying that they had overcome duality and become the embodiment of cosmic intelligence, the divine creative force.

As Jim Berenholtz puts it in *The Story of Quetzalcoatl*, "Quetzalcoatl, the plumed serpent, is the heart and essence of ancient America, representing the duality within and around all things in this universe." Evolution is achieved not by denying one side of reality in favor of the other, says Berenholtz, but by joining and interweaving both in harmonious balance.

In order to grasp the message contained in the appearance of the plumed serpent in Mesoamerica, it must be remembered that all periods of time and all divisions of space in sky and Earth were regarded as cosmic forces directed by and represented as gods.

One interesting fact of American history is that Hernando Cortez appeared among the Maya on the very year prophesied for Quetzalcoatl's return, after the deposition of the King of Tollan because of his opposition to human sacrifice, according to Frank Waters in *Mexico Mystique*. It is my belief that this event was only one facet of the Quetzalcoatl return—the one dealing with the karmic memory bank of post-Islamic Spain and the gory phase of Aztec human sacrifice. This atonement, I believe, resulted in the Mexican culture of today.

In order to see another side of the complex myth of Quetzalcoatl, it is important to realize what Waters reveals in his chapter on the feathered serpent in *Mexico Mystique*. He says the Nahuatl name comes from two words: *quetzal*, meaning "rare bird," and *coatl*, meaning "serpent." However, the word *coatl* is a combination of the generic Mayan term *co* for "serpent" and *atl*, meaning "water" or "twin brother." So Quetzalcoatl also may be translated as "the precious twin," a concept believed to have originated with the perception that the morning and evening stars are one and the same: Venus.

Looking now at the Hopi concept of Pahana, we find many similarities, especially in the concept of the sacred twins. The word "Pahana" comes from the root word *Pasu*, which means "salt water." In

Hopi, the concept of the feathered serpent is embodied in the word *palulukang*, which means "water serpent"—clearly an indication of Nahuatl origins.

Waters has a wonderful way of expressing this concept. As he puts it, "This may illustrate the old belief that Latin America will fulfill its true destiny only when the plumed serpent learns to fly."

In the search for clues about the return of Quetzalcoatl, we should keep in mind two other considerations: namely, that Quetzalcoatl is also called the "wind god" and that he promises to return from the east by way of the sea.

As an indication that Quetzalcoatl resides in each of us, I offer the following poem by Jim Berenholtz, written in Chichén Itzá, Mexico, on March 21, 1981:

> When,
> in all places,
> his belly is upon the ground,
> his spine upon the sky,
> and the core of his being
> lies equally between the two worlds
> of North and South,
> > Day and Night,
> > Heaven and Earth,
> > Woman and Man,
> When at once he shines
> as the Morning and the Evening Star,
> Look upon your Heart
> and you will see him,
> Quetzalcoatl.
>
> Do not shudder or turn away,
> for it is the time of Becoming.
> Open yourself
> Give yourself.
> Let him wave within you
> to feel the split
> that no longer exists.
> Your two halves are One.

Now let us look at the return of the Hopi Pahana. To do this, it will be necessary to bring to light some little-known Hopi writings. I would like to quote first from a letter written by Hopi elder Thomas Banyacya on behalf of the Independent Hopi Nation of the Village of Hotevilla. Acting at the time as a spokesman for village chief Dan Katchongva, Banyacya's letter truly expresses the thinking of all traditional Hopi:

> It is known that our true white brother, when he comes, will be all powerful and he will wear a red cap and a red cloak. He will be large in population and belong to no other religion than his very own. He will bring with him the sacred stone tablets. Great will be his coming. None will be able to stand against him.
>
> With him will be two great ones. One will have the sign symbol of the swastika, which for us represents the male energy, along with the sign of the cross, which is female. . . . It is also known that he will wear a cap similar to the back of a horned toad. . . .
>
> The second one of the two helpers will have a sign or a symbol of the sun. He too will be many people. We Hopis have in our sacred Katchina ceremonies a gourd rattle still in use today upon which the signs of these two powerful helpers are painted.

This is the Hopi description of the days of "purification," as they call it. In these passages, first we learn that the true Pahana is not a single personality but "large in population," a statement made earlier about Quetzalcoatl. This large population could include, I believe, the arrival of the Tibetan spiritual community. Tibetan rinpoches and lamas fit quite well the description in the Hopi prophecy.

In fact, a delegation of Tibetan lamas went to Hopi several years ago to meet with the traditional Hopi elders, with the intention of comparing prophecies. They met in David Monongye's kiva in what could be described only as a historical encounter. Also, the Dalai Lama came to Los Angeles a few years ago and gave audience to a number of Native American elders, among whom was Thomas Banyacya.

Similarities between the Tibetan lamas and the Hopi indicate that there has been some mysterious spiritual communication between the groups, in spite of their being geographically located on opposite sides of the planet. And there are similarities in language and ritual— especially the making of sand paintings as a healing and meditation device. The Tibetans also wear red capes and red or yellow caps, fit-ting the description of the people for whom the Hopi are waiting.

In Thomas Banyacya's letter we also learn that the swastika and the rising sun (symbols of Hitler's Germany and the Japanese during World War II) are indeed associated with the return of Pahana. This places the expectation of the return somewhere toward the end of the twentieth century.

Finally, the returning white brother will have to identify himself by returning the piece of the sacred stone tablet that he took with him when he left, as in the Hopi version of the creation myth. It is not clear whether this is to happen factually or symbolically.

For its part, the Indo-European world is awaiting fulfillment of its prophecies with anxieties similar to those of Mesoamerica. In Eastern and Western Europe there seems to be an attempt to fulfill an ancient prophecy that this part of the world will see the rebirth of Charlemagne's empire. As the European Common Market grows in strength and effectiveness toward a new "United States of Europe," the prophesied Austro-Hungarian "Holy Roman Empire" becomes a greater reality by the day. In fact, a powerful United States of Europe would also align well with prophecies for a future united planet.

Is this myth of the Second Coming consistent with present-day reality? Yes. Whether these almost identical myths were imported or whether they arose spontaneously in different forms from the collective unconscious, the fact is that the planet is now vibrating with readiness for transformation. Whichever of these many myths one chooses to examine, the messages of all are essentially the same. We are all looking into the heavens from different angles, but we all see the same star.

WERNEKE © 1990

The Second Coming: When?

It is not my intention to put more emphasis than necessary on present-day humanity's crisis. It is necessary, though, to emphasize that the Hopi "world out of balance" is not a fiction of the imagination but a reality to be reckoned with. In short, if we can convince ourselves of the urgency of the situation, we might convince ourselves to do something about it.

Humanity may well be nearing a point when planetary catastrophes become commonplace. For example, our atmosphere is in the worst shape ever in human history—as are the rain forests, the oceans, the rivers, and the land itself. As a result of our thoughtlessness, the very climate is changing, and it is likely that in the years ahead we will reap our just rewards in the form of droughts and food shortages.

Another "worst," of course, is the population problem. In the 1920s, the world's population was three billion. Sixty years later it is close to six billion—one billion in China alone. When viewed in terms of the available food supply alone, this is a frightening statistic.

Then there are the plagues that scourge humanity in different parts of the world. The recent droughts in Africa and even the United States and Russia have been called the worst in this century. AIDS is perhaps the worst and most lethal epidemic the planet has known, and it promises to become even more widespread. And how long can our present worldwide financial system continue in its present state of debt before it collapses under enormous sums of money that can never be repaid?

I would like to mention two other "worsts": Chernobyl, the worst nuclear catastrophe since the dropping of the atom bomb on Hiroshima and Nagasaki, and the devasting earthquake that shook

Soviet Armenia in 1988, killing fifty thousand people.

In my view, these and other "worst" scenarios indicate that the world is far beyond Band-Aid medicine. In a time when it is clear that national interests must immediately be sacrificed for the good of all, I see little evidence of worldwide cooperation to solve these problems. Even the faint voice of the United Nations cannot be heard above the collective dissent. It is clear that we can no longer get back on course by ourselves. More than ever, we need help from the Cosmos. I believe humanity is about to get that help and that the remedy will be as painful as it is helpful.

As I see it, the way to deal with these and other impending problems is not to sink into depression, but to realize that the world is "in labor." There is a birthing going on, not a death. Exactly when the birth will take place is hard to predict, but let us remember that the labor pains in any birth are painful and tend to accelerate as the happy time draws near. In order to determine the actual time of the birth, then, we have to consider the frequency and severity of the labor pains.

Perhaps one compensation is that through these labor pains the world is being purified as it passes through the end of the present cycle. The process is much like that of gold, which comes from the earth as an ore mixed with many impurities, then passes through a series of crucibles under temperatures up to fourteen hundred degrees Fahrenheit before it becomes the gleaming pure gold we recognize and value.

But what of the actual time of the cleansing, the purification, the return of the savior and helpful brother? If Christ, Quetzalcoatl, Kukulcan, and Pahana all represent a new consciousness rather than actual personalities, when will they manifest in the lives of human beings?

One solid body of information we have about the actual time of the Second Coming is the comparative descriptions of "the last days" found in various religious works. These descriptions lean toward the idea that the last days will be a "phase" of human evolution rather than actual days—an era, cycle, or *katun*, as the Maya would say.

I believe it is also relevant to recall a very unusual event that took place in the little mountain village of Fatima in Portugal. There, three young shepherds reported that "a beautiful lady"—a lady who seemed to them to be "heavenly"—appeared on a spring day in 1916 and stayed through October 13, 1917, talking to them about world events.

After insisting that they should pray for Russia (the Russian Revolution was also in 1917), she left them with this enigmatic statement: "In the end, Russia will be converted." In light of the democratization that is now occurring in Russia and its satellites as the last decade of the century begins, this statement is, I believe, another indication that "the last days" are here.

Considering such sources as the Bible, Nostradamus, and Toltec, Zapotec, Chichimec, Mayan, and Incan texts, as well as current world events, I think it is reasonable to say that the Second Coming—the transformation of the planet through the Christ energy—will occur gradually during the last part of this century and the early part of the next. In other words, we are in the "last days" right now, though many are too blind to recognize the fact.

WERNEKE © 1990

CHAPTER 9

Can Humanity Regain Control of Its Destiny?

The Hopi describe today's situation as a "world out of balance." The New Age culture calls it a "world in transformation." The scientific community might call it a "world in evolution." In any case, people all over the world are becoming aware that the great changes can no longer be pushed aside or ignored. But just where are these changes taking us? What kind of lives might we create for ourselves after the birth of the new world? I believe part of the answer lies in the ways of the Native Americans.

Toward the end of the last century, the Paiute seer Wowoka became entangled in the last significant revolt of the Plains Indians against their American oppressors. His numerous visions led to the creation of a native religious revival called the Ghost Dance. What Wowoka saw in his visions was a peaceful ceremonial dance of all the races of the world. However, it was interpreted by the defeated tribes as a war dance that would liberate them from their oppressors. The Ghost Dance revival ended at Wounded Knee, where white soldiers massacred the Cheyennes in their camp—men, women, and children alike.

But was Wounded Knee really the end of the Native American influence on this continent? Not at all. At the present time, the world is witnessing a major revival of Native American philosophy, ceremonialism, and cultural influence.

This revival has taken two forms. First, the Indian people themselves are taking greater pride in their own culture. And second, a growing body of white Americans are discovering and adopting the grace and wisdom in native ceremonies and lifeways. Some observers of this phenomenon believe that many of these white Americans are the reincarnations of natives who were slaughtered in the name of progress and who have come back to help reestablish a balance on the globe. My own observations lead me to conclude that this movement is indeed part of the "return." In any case, growing numbers of people are coming to see native lifeways and attitudes as hopeful means of regaining control over their lives.

One of the most attractive elements in native life, and one that undoubtedly will play a major role in the new balanced world, is intuition. Reasoning and intellect have taken center stage in the modern scientific world, while intuition has been suspect. Yet man lived successfully for thousands of years guided primarily by his inner voice, and there is good reason to believe that it will be a primary tool in regaining control and balance in our lives.

Let us quickly look at some of the other factors that will be necessary for humanity to regain control of its destiny. First and foremost is a protection for the Earth that flows from true respect and love. Second, I would say, is the ability of nations to cooperate in solving worldwide problems such as acid rain, air and water pollution, and nuclear waste. The inhabitants of a planet threatened with annihilation have no choice but to clean up the mess they have created. If the nations of Planet Earth are incapable or unwilling to cooperate with each other, then catastrophe is inevitable.

I believe that the "cleanup" will take place anyway—if necessary, without sparing humankind. The geological layers of the Earth's crust give credence to the fact that such global cleanups have taken place before, probably reducing the human population enormously each time. Hope that this might not happen again resides in the fact that humankind could use its technical abilities to mount a "save the planet" drive. This is where a little push from the returning Pahana might seem likely, to make humanity more conscious of its responsibilities.

It seems likely that the conduit for such a behavior change would be the hundredth-monkey principle—the awakening of a sufficient number of people on the planet so as to cause a shift in sensibility that results in positive action and international cooperation. Somehow, all nations need to be convinced of the need to purify the environment and rebalance the biosphere. In a word, this is the greatest challenge ever faced by humanity.

On the other hand, humankind is a social collective. We have used collective cooperation countless times before to solve problems that seemed insurmountable. Great construction projects such as the pyramids, countless castles and fortifications, the Great Wall of China, and modern office towers have been built with such cooperation. Of course, many of these projects were built with slave labor, and there will be no forced enrollment this time.

In the past our selfish, egotistical behavior has fueled the notion of "more profit with less effort." It has been this attitude that has contributed largely to the building of today's monolithic and materialistic society. Tomorrow's drive must be spiritualized or it will fail. Nothing less than a respiritualization of human behavior will save humanity from roasting in the "greenhouse," drying up lakes, spoiling the seas, killing the trees, making the Earth into a parched desert that is incapable of feeding its inhabitants. Nothing less than a global effort of monumental proportions can accomplish a miracle of this scope. And our cooperation had better begin soon, because the clock is ticking. What we need is a worldwide "Harmonic Convergence" of ideas and efforts.

In my view, part of the return of Pahana, or the Christ, or Quetzalcoatl, in these critical times is the return of an earthly "cycle" that will incorporate the qualities mankind needs most: faith, compassion, and love instead of greed, selfishness, and illegitimate profit. This will be a cycle that operates on principles that have characterized the great spiritual teachers of all time. Looking back, humans will have only to see the destruction created by the previous cycle to gather their energies to move ahead.

The message of the return is here, now, revealed in the content of everyday life. It is perhaps cloudy at the moment, but still it waits to be urged forward through the presence of a returning archetype that will redirect the efforts that have been consumed in so many wrong choices and have led to such despair.

This is where the Native American revival, the New Age revolution, and the hundredth-monkey syndrome are taking us. This is what the return is all about: the myth becoming reality.

If the circumstances of life on the planet are observed carefully, then we might have to agree with the Maya that we are all racing to the end of a huge cycle and preparing to enter a new one. It is imperative that we all prepare ourselves to enter this next great wheel, as the "new world" is already knocking on our doors.

We all have a responsibility in this. Part of that responsibility is to see the elements of the return with clarity. The New Age society in formation, yesterday's American Indians in today's white man's clothing, the renewed native consciousness, the Tibetan gift of dharma to the West—all these and more can be viewed as integral parts of the Hopi stone tablet that is being brought back by Pahana. The time has arrived when everyone must give something to the process of transformation. That is the only way we can all survive.

What is needed is individualism at the service of collective regrouping. When fire fighters are battling a blazing forest, they go back home to rest only after the fire is over. As we all fight the fire together, a new humanity will emerge from the ashes and new patterns of behavior will be created. Instead of going to church one hour each Sunday, the entirety of life will once again become a prayer, an act of faith. To love our enemies as ourselves will become the motto for everyday living, not because such an attitude will enrage our enemies but because it will enhance the growth and development of all.

This new consciousness will permeate public life as it enhances private life. Everything will be touched by it: politics, economics, finance, religion, and personal relationships.

This is the fire we will all be fighting together, the fire that for all of us will signify the collective "return." This we will do for personal and collective survival. But we will also do it with new enthusiasm and understanding, for we will be burning with a renewed internal fire, with a new understanding of the life plan set forth by the Creator.

At times, fighting the fire together, some of us will get burned. But we must all realize that as one cycle ends, the next one has already begun. We must prepare ourselves to be even closer to the original divine plan. This is the meaning of spiritual evolution. This is the meaning of the Second Coming, the return of Pahana.

Followers of the Tibetan Buddhist dharma believe that Sakyamuni Gautama Buddha, returns to life in every monk, lama, and rinpoche who practices the faith. In this clear and simple approach, the return of the archetype is a constant happening. This gives a permanence to the dogma of salvation implied by the supernatural return.

As we all fight the fire that threatens to engulf humanity, as we all become fused in the crucible of purification, we will become truer to ourselves and to others, clearer in our minds about the roles given each of us as we enter and reenter life through the revolving door of birth and death. What looms on the horizon as the most terrible experience of all—the potential death of humanity—could become a transformation for humanity if we seize the opportunity to regain control of our destiny.

Specific hope of this possibility is offered in the recent democratization of the Communist Bloc countries. Democracy does not have all the answers, of course, but at least it offers a political climate that allows people to breathe and provide for their own basic needs. As this text is written, the stifling grip of Communism is loosening in Eastern Europe and China. This is nothing short of a political miracle. It was made possible, I believe, by the worldwide shift of energies that heralds the return of Pahana.

I believe it is also true that the way we live on this plane affects the way we will live in the great Unknown. In other words, for those of us who believe in reincarnation, there is a direct connection between our actions in this life and what happens to us in our next life. We also can consciously influence the quality of our next life by our actions in the present moment. What better way to insure the quality of future lives for all than to take control of our destiny right now?

One of the ways we can regain control of our destiny is to reduce our dependencies. Whether drugs, cars, sex, cigarettes, junk food, or various emotional dependencies, addictions destroy true freedom of the individual. Once we are hooked on one or more of the above, we become easier prey to scams, get-rich-quick schemes, political manipulations, and our own worst passions.

Of course, many of these addictions are fostered and promoted by the corporate world, a world that deifies competition and profit. It is my belief that the new energies, as they purify individuals, will also purify and transform the world's major institutions, from corporations to banks and government agencies.

The Hopi call the purified and strengthened world of tomorrow the "Fifth World." To the Hopi, three previous worlds have already passed away. We are presently living at the end of the fourth. To the

Hopi, then, the "end of the world," like the end of a life, is only a new beginning. For us all to have this awareness would be a tremendous step forward for humanity—much more significant than an astronaut walking on the moon. It would signal the expansion of human consciousness and a quickening of our spiritual evolution.

Native societies have an intuitive knowledge that modern man has largely lost. Part of their innate awareness is a deep understanding of the role the Earth has played in the functioning of the universe. Ask the average man on the street if he knows what the Earth's role in the universe is, and brace yourself for a dumbfounded stare. Someday soon, everyone will know about our planet's place in the cosmos. Such knowledge is essential to the full meaning of life.

The great monuments of native societies the world over represent mystical and esoteric truths. I would venture to say that more than ninety percent of the metaphysical knowledge implied by these monuments has been lost. In order for humanity to regain control of its destiny, such knowlege somehow must be rekindled.

Fortunately, there is a little bit of Christ, Pahana, Quetzalcoatl, and Kukulcan in everyone. The human mind harbors the sum total of the genetic history of the whole of humanity. This fact in itself, when combined with the present crisis, should be enough to trigger our common responsibility.

Speaking of responsibility, I believe it is possible that today's New Age subculture—in particular those individuals who embrace Native American ways—might well represent an opportunity for the pioneers of the American past to repay their karmic debt to those they slaughtered in their push to settle the West. It is also possible that the New Age represents the vision of Wowoka, the Paiute seer who saw peoples of different colors and cultures dancing together. At any rate, both the Hopi and most of the Puebloan world of the American Southwest believe that the problems of today's non-Indian world are related to this karmic situation.

As the Hopi myth predicts, Pahana, the elder white brother of the Hopi, is supposed to appear through the clouds to help resolve this great world crisis. It is he who is supposed to give both white and red brothers a new chance to walk the original path of the Creator, the path of brotherhood, compassion, and humility. Once this choice has been made, the path of selfishness and greed that has led the four previous worlds to their destruction will have been abandoned at last, and we will truly live in a world transformed.

The last twelve years of this century and the first twelve or fourteen of the next will be especially crucial for paving the way from one cycle to the next, the Fourth World to the fifth. Christian, pre-Christian and Mesoamerican predictions, along with the mathematical calculations of the Maya that have predicted a new era, all point toward this truth. Clearly, the native world has anticipated these events, as their oral, written, and hieroglyphic traditions so eloquently testify. It is now the responsibility of our modern industrial and technological society to grasp the true meaning of the term "world out of balance," to understand what has triggered this situation and how we can use this knowledge to reestablish world harmony.

My contacts over the years with native societies, especially the Hopi and Pueblos, have made me keenly aware of the native approach to the continuum of history. It is because of the knowledge I have acquired from these people that I have undertaken the complex presentation that is the essence of this book.

It is not an easy matter to talk and write about the unrealized facts of the future. Nevertheless, I believe the mythic concept of the Second Coming and the return of Quetzalcoatl and Pahana to be absolutely plausible. As historians tell us, the future is a time capsule that waits to be unlocked. But as seers of all times and places have amply demonstrated, it can be decoded by those who have the unusual ability to look through time.

Trusting predictions and prophecies is just as important as interpreting the past. Trusting that prophecies of the world's future from different times and places all point in the same direction, perhaps, will make it easier for us to do the only decent thing left for us to do—and that is simply to have faith.

WERNEKE © 1990

E P I L O G U E

It is the time of the yearly Mayan spring equinox initiation, and a long line of young men have prepared themselves for the great religious event in the temple of Chac-mol. The men have come from throughout the district. Adorned in pure white vestments, they wear headbands of different colors to indicate the villages of their origins.

The pristine air of early morning is scented with wildflowers. The Sun Father will not come out to preside over the scheduled events for another hour.

Walking slowly and reverently, the men bow their heads toward the Earth in constant meditation. This contingent of supplicants moves in two lines on both sides of the great road leading to the heart of the sacred city of Uxmal. Arms loaded with bouquets of flowers to be offered to the sacred women, they pray.

In a huge compound called the nunnery, the female participants have prepared themselves for the initiation, just as the men did at the religious center of Ka-Bah, miles away.

Tensions run high as the men approach the sanctuary. None of them knows whether the sacred women will even want to greet them, as custom requires in order for the ceremony to be complete. The whole ceremony is designed to honor the divine role of the sexes in the sacred ways of the Maya.

Sequestered in their quarters for the last three days, great deliberations have taken place among the corps of women in order to decide the proper time for the greeting, or even whether it will be proper at all for the men to be initiated into the ways of the women. If the council of women elders decides to do so, then and only then will the men be led into the nunnery where they will participate in the sacred tantric ceremony—for men and women are partners in creation.

At the gate, the men stand still, two long lines of anxious worshipers. Suddenly, from the steps of the round pyramid of Uxmal, a pyramid unique in the Mayan world, they see a female envoy coming slowly down toward them. She leaves a written message.

The men's council of elders approaches to discover the contents of the message. It is a riddle. In order to be accepted into the women's sanctuary, the men must decode it successfully. The riddle tells of an insensitive warrior who has violated the women's sensitivity and honor. It is an indication of the skeptical mood of the women in the nunnery.

The oldest of the men, as president of the council, suggests answering the women's distrust with love and compassion. He feels the women will honor these gentle sentiments. His intuition proves to be right. When the women's messenger returns a second time, the men learn that greetings and acceptance are awaiting them.

The men's long-contained expectation now explodes with shouts of joy, and huge conch shells are blown with enough power and enthusiasm to be heard throughout the immense jungle that surrounds the sacred city.

Preceded by perhaps a dozen of the men blowing the sacred conch shells, the long white line of men proceeds slowly toward the inner sanctum of the nunnery. The spectacle awaiting them is beyond words. In each of the trapezoidal doors that open to the enormous plaza stands a woman dressed in white. Each wears a red headband. The long white robes of the women seem irridescent as the men approach the main entrance. Arms folded over their chests, the women look like angelic figures from another dimension. Indeed, a new dimension will pervade every moment, every gesture during this expression of the initiation ritual the men have come so far to receive.

As the men enter the central square of the nunnery, they discover that every opening is adorned with a sacred woman wearing virginal white robes. The men form a huge circle as they enter, depositing bouquets of flowers at the main shrine.

The head of the women elders council stands in front of the shrine. The moment is awesome. There is no doubt in anyone's mind that this elderly woman, standing before an altar resplendent with flowers, is the physical symbol of the universal mother.

At this point, in slow motion, the entire body of female celebrants begins to form a circle totally surrounding the circle of men. Everyone joins hands. Then begins a most amazing ritual, with both circles slowly and majestically revolving in opposite directions. The men move counterclockwise, the women clockwise.

Everyone involved in this sacred tantric exercise, this ritual dance of love, is pervaded with feelings of ecstasy—especially so because each woman has been instructed to stare into each man's eyes as the slowly moving circle places each one in front of the other. The instant transports each of the men into an etheric dimension, another world permeated with sexual energy.

As the ritual continues, its participants lose all awareness of space and time. Toward the end, the two circles fuse with one another, one celebrant of each gender holding the hand of his or her opposite. The long line finally moves in one direction in a snakelike motion. The endless snake undulates its way toward wholeness and bliss, the ultimate purpose of the initiation.

The spring equinox festival has not quite been completed, however. The final celebration has been scheduled for the following day in the Mayan-Toltec sacred city of Chichén Itzá, miles away. This last phase of the initiation occurs when the long line of initiates, just as in Uxmal, encircles the main pyramid and temple, singing and dancing in the same snakelike fashion as during the previous day. The initiates are honoring the return of Kukulcan, symbolized by the mysterious shadowy projection of a gigantic snake down the entire side of the huge pyramid. It is a solemn moment when the rays of the setting sun project this form of the returning god. Every one of the fifty thousand people assembled seems transfixed by the apparition.

Finally, the great crowd of worshipers sings in unison to the god: "Kukulcan, Kukulcan, Kukulcan. . .Meshico, Meshico, Meshico. . ."

———————————

It is close to noon on a hot summer's day at the Hopi mesa called Shipaulovi. A stone's throw from the village, on a small rocky ledge called Soyok Mesa, a man lies flat on a slab of sandstone. His face is bathed in the light of Tawa, the Sun Father. He appears very tired from walking in the fields below. He is just about to fall asleep for a short nap before lunch.

But then, in the twilight of his fading consciousness, the man sees an unusually tall figure appear before him. The figure is that of a huge man, perhaps ten feet tall, extremely slender, and with long blond hair cascading to his shoulders. He is dressed all in white. Surprisingly, his features are not Indian, but Caucasian.

Startled, the sleepy man asks, "Who are you?" "I am Somiviki," answers the apparition, then goes on to tell the man only a few words more. "You will have your own clan," he says. "It will be called the Banana Clan." With that, the apparition disappears as suddenly as it came.

The man awakens fully and ponders his amazing vision. Somiviki, he knows, is a ritual foodstuff resembling a Mexican tamale, prepared with blue cornmeal and ashes and used solely for ceremonial purposes. Bananas, however, are unknown to the Hopi.

What is the meaning of all this? The man wonders. Was the giant human figure perhaps the spirit of Pahana as the white brother would appear in physical form? Was he a kachina? And the message about a Banana Clan—was this some sort of cosmic joke? The man is certain the apparition said, "Banana," not "Bahanna" or "Pahana." It simply does not make sense.

———————————

Why did I choose to tell these two stories in the epilogue of this book? Because they are not just stories; they are real events, recounted as they actually happened. And they happened to me.

When I went to the Yucatán in the spring of 1989, I had in mind to study carefully the possibility that the Hopi myth of the Red City of the South, or "Ba-lát-quah-bi," as it is called in Hopi, might be a historical fact. I joined a party of almost a hundred people—a party that at times swelled to 150—under the sponsorship of a Mayan elder by the name of Hunbatz Men. This pilgrimage to Mayan sacred cities, temples, and pyramids was called "Mayan Initiation Centers for the Year 2013." Indeed, it was a mystical initiation in every sense, involving all of us in daily ceremonies and ritualistic endeavors.

My personal search to find the Red City was also rewarded. I can now say with certainty that Ba-lát-quah-bi is the city of Palenque. The Maya call it the city of Nah-Chan. Some of the Hopi kachina masks still in use today in Hopi ceremonies can be found on stelae, temples, and pyramids, and on the tombstone of Pacal, the lord and high priest of Nah-Chan. Some bas-reliefs portray priests offering kachina dolls smoking tubular pipes identical to those still used in modern kiva ceremonies at Hopi.

Although trying to keep my findings in rational perspective, I must say that intuitively (and I have learned through the years to trust my intuition) I know that some of the Hopi clans originally came from Mayan country, bringing with them on their long migrations the fathers of all kachinas, Eototo and Aholi.

The tantric ceremony I described was not an ancient Mayan event, but a modern-day enactment exactly as it was conducted in the Mayan sacred city of Uxmal in the spring of 1989. Never have I been more convinced that the ancient spirits of Quetzalcoatl and Kukulcan are indeed returning to our planet.

As for what happened to me at Hopi, it must sound like fiction. Yet the circumstances and the vision were exactly as I described them. It all happened on a hot summer day in 1950, right across from the village of Shipaulovi on a small, rocky mesa.

In the years following my vision, I visited the Hopi frequently. Spontaneously, my Hopi family and friends began referring to my non-Hopi friends as "Bananas"—a humorous play on the Hopi word "Bahanna," or "Pahana," meaning white man. As the years passed, I became inspired to gather some of these mostly white men and women together and pass on to them some of the ceremonial ways I had been taught at Hopi.

Gradually, I discovered that we were indeed forming a clan of our own—a non-Hopi group with its own unique expression, but a group spiritually rooted in Hopi soil. Who knows—perhaps the Banana Clan, one of many groups today that respect and embrace Native American ways, embodies some of the spirit of Pahana himself. Some things still remain a great mystery.

At any rate, for many years—in fact, until I took my trip to the Yucatán in the spring of 1989—I never knew why the tall blond figure in my vision had used the word "Banana" when bananas do not even grow at Hopi. Now I know. Bananas grow everywhere in the Yucatán. They even grow out of the streets! This is something I could not have known when the visionary experience occurred. But Somiviki, essence of the blue corn, sacred food of the Hopi, undoubtedly knew that the banana had once been a sacred symbol. Perhaps it was the totem fruit of a clan that lived in Palenque when groups now called Hopi were an integral part of the Mayan complex tribal organization.[11]

One consolation at the time of my unexplained vision was the wonderful reaction of the Hopi family with whom I was living. They took the whole sequence of events very seriously. They also laughed a lot about it, which in the Hopi way means not only that they found it funny, but that they understood the meaning of it all.

That meaning was to escape me for many years—almost forty, to be exact. Only then did I establish the connection, as though I myself were a Maya of some previous incarnation returning home in another day, another time.

————————

Hunbatz Men, the Mayan spiritual leader who organized the Mayan Initiation 2013 and who acted as high priest during the Yucatán trip, proved to be somewhat of a magician. For example, in the sacred center of Chichén Itzá, he predicted that he and his "pilgrims" (ourselves) would soon "move" fifty thousand people.

Nobody understood what he meant until the next day, when, in front of the Mexican militia and fifty thousand spectators, he led us in a sublime dance in which everyone joined hands around the huge pyramid of Kukulcan.

Hunbatz also had repeatedly mentioned to us certain Mayan prophecies predicting that the ancient Maya themselves would come back to reoccupy their sacred cities and religious centers at the end of the present cycle. Much to our amazement, we discovered that some of these ancient Maya were ourselves—or at least that we, the pilgrims of the twentieth century, represented the symbolic return of these Maya.

Having previously known and accepted all this with complete faith, Hunbatz had organized this group of about 150 of us from all parts of the world. Having done so, he proceeded to create a society modeled after that of the ancient Maya themselves. As with the Maya of old, the nucleus of power behind our group was the Council of Elders. Its membership was based on age and wisdom, and its decisions became instant law.

During our two weeks of ceremonies and rituals in the Yucatán, we operated entirely on this basis. The Council of Elders made all the decisions, and the rest of the group implemented those decisions without question.

At the end of our stay in the sacred Mayan centers, however, we wondered whether the Council of Elders was meant to survive. If indeed on some level we represented a group of Maya whose spirits had returned to fulfill the prophecies, then somehow it seemed only natural that the council should remain operative.

Not surprisingly, it soon occurred to us to meet again, to discuss future plans for our newly formed "Neo-Mayan" society. Accordingly, we decided that sometime following the trip we *would* have another meeting of the Council of Elders.

But where would it be?

When people are living and acting naturally outside the artificial fabric of time, answers often come without hesitation or conflict. The proper place to nourish the tree whose roots we had discovered in the Mayan temples was immediately obvious to all of us. We would meet again at Hopi!

Even in terms of my vision of 1950, this decision made perfect sense. None of us realized it at the time, but I later had the distinct sense that our decision had been triggered by the spirit of the original migration from the Mayan sacred sites to Hopi more than a thousand years before. Now, once again, it seemed, that same migration was about to take place in symbolic form.

It also occurred to me that all of this must have been conceived far beyond the realm of the "ordinary" human mind. Only in this way could our journeys take their proper place in the fabric of prophecy. Now, without consciously realizing it, our little group of elders was about to reenact the ancient mythical migrations of the Hopi themselves.

Thus, between July 28 and August 1, 1989, the "Mayan-Hopi-Banana" connection was finally made. And everything fell into place with remarkable synchronicity. For example, while I was planning the trip, I had no way of knowing the exact date of the last ceremony of the Hopi kachina calendar. Nevertheless, the arrival of the Council of Elders at Hopi coincided exactly with the last kachina ceremonial of the year. This was remarkable also because the ceremonial took place in Shipaulovi, the village where I once lived and near which the original Banana Clan shrine is located.

Unwittingly I had planned for our arrival to coincide with this sacred Hopi ceremony. And so it happened. I felt as if the Great Spirit were indicating in no uncertain terms that the Mayan-Hopi connection was not just in our minds, but was in fact reality.

No longer do the Maya have ceremonies comparable to those of the Hopi. These were discontinued after the arrival of the conquistadors in the sixteenth century, when Spanish authorities forbade their being held. By contrast, the Hopi have been performing their kachina ceremonies uninterruptedly for more than a thousand years.

Assuming that at least some of the present-day Hopi are descendants of the ancient Maya, does this mean that some of the Mayan rituals have been preserved by the Hopi? Are some of today's Hopi kachina dances modern enactments of ceremonies once performed by the ancient Maya themselves? In my opinion, this is very likely so.

With this perspective, when one considers that ancient religious centers literally cover the American Southwest, the sacred dances and ceremonies of the Hopi, Zuni, and Pueblos of the Rio Grande take on huge historical proportions. Collectively, these ceremonies are probably living testimony to the religious splendor of ancient societies that most people believe have left behind only "ruins." Even ruins are rich with life and memory. Each time I watch a kachina ritual on the Hopi mesas, this thought takes precedence over all others.

So it was that our little group was blessed to witness the "Niman," the annual "going home" ceremony of the Hopi kachinas. The ceremony began shortly after six o'clock in the morning. I remember the scene as the sun was just about to appear on the eastern horizon. We could still feel the coolness of the night hours; however, a crowd had already filled every available space on the village's central plaza. Most of the spectators were Hopi from the little village itself or those who had come from surrounding villages to watch the ceremony.

Suddenly, breaking the silence and the drowsiness of the crowd, a group of forty-four masked supernatural beings appeared on the western side of the square. These were the "Long-Hair Kachinas." Their bodies were painted black. Each wore a blue mask with long black hair. Each also wore a short, handwoven kilt called a *pitchkuni*, brown moccasins, a turtle shell fastened to one leg, and bells on the other leg. The arms of the kachinas were full of corn plants.

The crowd, which had by now overflowed onto the rooftops, was silent, completely overcome by the sight of the kachinas.

After piling the corn plants at the center of the plaza, the forty-four kachinas formed a long line on the south side of the square. Then they began to move—slowly, rhythmically. Each footstep and body movement was in perfect time with all the others, as well as with the accompanying chanting and drumming.

As in previous years, the experience was awesome. Nowhere else have I seen rituals duplicated with such religious, choreographic, and musical splendor. Many times while witnessing such ceremonies I have been overcome and fallen into a trance, lifted into other realms by the compelling combination of sound and vision. Small wonder I call the Hopi the mystics of the desert!

The dance went on all day, interrupted only by short rest periods during which the kachinas retreated into a cave located under one of the nearby cliffs. There, during the rest periods, the kachinas loaded themselves up with gifts for the Hopi families attending the event. Then they freely doled out kachina dolls for the little girls, bows and arrows for the little boys, and mountains of foodstuffs for the grown-ups.

As the sun went down in the west, the ceremony ended in a much smaller plaza. There, in a small circle, the kachinas were blessed by their priests and priestesses, who had come through the roof opening of a nearby kiva. Finally, these spiritual leaders gave the kachinas a farewell address in Hopi, ceremonially "sending them out" toward the San Francisco peaks above Flagstaff, Arizona, their spiritual home. The kachinas would return at the end of the year, when another ceremonial, called Soyal, would bring them back to the villages for another season of festivities.

All this was beautiful to behold. However, as the fabric of life is woven in opposites, I was not surprised that the ceremony was marred by a form of negativity that gave some of us pause for reflection.

As we watched the last kachina performance of the day, one of our number on the roof pointed and called my attention to something she saw at the edge of the plaza. To my great consternation, I saw three members of our group outfitted in the most outrageous costumes, including bells and pheasant feathers, apparently trying to match or compete with the splendor of the kachina ritual itself. My blood froze as I prayed they would not physically disrupt the dance.

Interestingly, nothing happened. The kachinas and Hopi spectators simply ignored the exhibitionists and went on with their ceremony. Yet anyone with even a little awareness of Hopi etiquette must have been struck by the arrogance of their intrusion. For the Hopi, whose very society is based on humility and respect for the ancient ways, the attempt of these three to call attention to themselves with their own personal parade must have been a real slap in the face.

Yet in reflecting on the event, I realized two things. One, the Hopi are used to such behavior from outsiders. Rather than treating it as an affront, they are humble enough to ignore it as a form of ignorance. And second, rarely do ceremonial events go off without a hitch. For every action, there is a reaction. And however embarrassing it was to us, I realized that on another level, several of our members had simply helped to provide the dark thread in the tapestry.

Being thus greeted with this magnificent ceremony was an auspicious beginning to our spiritual pilgrimage to Hopi. The next major event was a visit to the Hopi sacred site called Prophecy Rock.

Situated near the ancient village of Oraibi, Prophecy Rock is a huge slab of stone standing two stories high and on which is engraved a pictograph illustrating the Hopi vision of the modern world. Carved into the rock are two symbolic paths. One is the deceptive route, characterized by materialism and confusion; the other is the path of the Great Spirit, characterized by the original instructions of prayer, honest labor, and spiritual understanding.

This stopover was valued for two reasons: first, because Hopi prophecy in recent years has played a prominent role in many a vision of the so-called "New World"; and second, because it was the perfect place to reflect and prepare us all for our subsequent visits with the Hopi themselves.

After our visit to Prophecy Rock, our little "Neo-Mayan" contingent had two important meetings with Hopi elders—elders who represent the two factions that collectively oversee the social, political, and economic life of the Hopi. These meetings included much serious as well as good-natured talk, not to mention delicious feasts of Hopi ceremonial foods. Yet beyond the talk and the food, I always felt the presence of the roots of Maya guiding and feeding our interactions.

To close the three days of the Hopi "Mayan Elders" conference, I had scheduled a sunrise ceremony at the shrine of the Banana Clan. Thus, on the last day of our visit, long before sunrise, we climbed the little rocky mesa where I had had my original vision.

The climb was a feast for the eyes as well as for the spirit. Located not far from the village of Shipaulovi, the small, rocky platform offered a most entrancing view of hundreds of square miles of Arizona desert. Far in the distance on that especially clear morning, I could see the San Francisco peaks, mythic home of the kachinas themselves. Much closer, the three peaks of the Hopi Buttes seemed to spring right out of the desert floor. With this magnificent backdrop, we faced the Hopi shrine of the Banana Clan with its slab of carved stone. And there Hunbatz Men performed a beautiful ceremony, greeting Tawa, the Sun Father, who had just risen into our line of vision. With this joyful communion between humans, Earth, and sky, I had the distinct feeling that the Mayan-Hopi-Banana connection was finally complete—and that soon, through events just as mysterious and wonderful as had befallen our little group, the world would be blessed with the return of Pahana.

*There can
be no tomorrow
as long as there is
today.*

Po Pai Mo

CONCLUSION

Messages for the Year 2000

The Return of Pahana no doubt raises as many questions as it answers. Not the least of these are questions about what kind of people we want to become and what kind of thinking will hasten and encourage the return of spiritual light on our planet and in our lives. With this in mind, I offer a collection of messages, or personal meditations, that I hope will contribute to your own personal awakening.

It is my conviction that we cannot move into the twenty-first century without a philosophy, a sociology, and a new mode of political thought that will work to truly nurture the human species. We need a new way of thinking. For this reason, too, I decided to include the following messages.

In a sense, these messages are not my own. I received them while sitting in meditation in an Indian kiva, an underground chamber in which Puebloan societies gather to pray and meditate. The messages came to me periodically throughout the year of 1983. As I became aware that they incorporated some worthwhile teaching, I started jotting them down.

To make all of this more intelligible, I would like to explain that the process of receiving these messages was one of "locution"; the messages did not go through the normal auditory channels but were transmitted and impressed directly into my mind and intellect. As I analyzed their content later on, I was frankly surprised by their depth and clarity, as well as by their sociological and philosophical implications. And while rereading them recently, I began to realize their importance in helping to master the understanding of the subject of this book: the return of the sacred archetype.

Humanity cannot embark on a new cycle with the same thinking that brought on the present state of confusion; our thinking must be brand new. In order to facilitate such new thinking, and to briefly summarize the messages that follow, I have synthesized here what appear to me to be the essential concepts, or hallmarks, of the New Age.

First of all, humanity's route to salvation lies in a return to the inherent dignity, priority, and strength of the individual. Institutions—even those that are benign and seemingly essential—nevertheless inherently contain a certain "demonic" quality.

The institutionalizing process tends, by its very nature, to dehumanize, consume, and, ultimately, destroy. This is the history of governments, economic and financial entities, and the like. One possible exception to this is the family, the cradle from which the individual rises to his or her destiny.

The world we live in today is prone to favor the collectivistic side of every aspect of human life. Education, business, finance, politics, and even religious organizations concentrate most of their efforts on the collective. In order to start reemphasizing the individual, we must stop idolizing the cult of the colossal.

Many societies before our own fell into the same trap, in which individuals, the human expressions of the power of creation on Earth, were seen more as parts of the whole than as institutions in their own right. Collective bodies and groups are extensions of the individuals who compose them; they are only as efficient and effective—and humane—as their individual members.

No institution can possibly claim to be "part of the process of creation." For institutions are, in fact, projections of the human mind into the realm of practicality. Their purpose is to give humanity protection and power. Unfortunately, the birth of the institution begins a "dehumanizing" process that entraps both the individual and his or her inherent capabilities.

In order to "re-humanize" the existence of every man, woman, and child, certain values must be taken into consideration. One of these is the purpose of human life. And if the purpose of human life is not to create huge social structures, then what is it?

As I see it, the purpose of human life is to face every experience, good or bad—including every struggle, every conflict, and every battle—with an eye toward expanding one's capacity for understanding: in other words, to learn.

When death comes, the only possession we will be allowed to take along with us will be the net result of our experiences. Therefore, it does not make much sense for us to spend great amounts of time and energy building monoliths or even nest eggs that will have to be left behind.

The watchword of the human experience in its corporeal state is "struggle." Trying to minimize that for which we are essentially here would be like taking the wheels off an automobile or the wings off a plane.

And what about "human rights"? Let it be known that the only human right we really have is to face the experiences of our lives on the basis of our abilities. No one can be held accountable for something he or she did not have the ability to do. Nor do personal freedom and unfoldment depend exclusively on "good" experiences. In time of peace or in time of war, in time of prosperity or in time of need, in sickness or in health, the chances of ultimate success—that is, for spiritual growth and learning—are identical for everyone, as they depend solely on the capabilities inherent in each individual. Equality between people is maintained by a formula that guarantees that we will not be held accountable for what we did not have the strength or ability to do.

This is part of what the word "humanity" means. But it is easy to see that on the collective level it cannot mean the same thing as it does for the individual. For on the collective level, it triggers the very "inhumanity" that endangers human society.

In the last hundred years, since the Age of the Great Inventions at the end of the nineteenth century, technology has pushed humanity relentlessly toward institutionalization. This has happened in every domain, minimizing the importance of the individual, the original cell. As a result, the chances for a balanced and integrated world have diminished accordingly.

Tensions and disagreements between institutions have increased to a point of almost no return, dragging the individual members of these collective bodies along with them and ending in a syndrome of despair—a catastrophic vision of the future that might be regarded as a chronic state of collective depression. Much of the world is gripped in an apocalyptic vision of holocaust, after which social organization would have to be started all over again by a humanity greatly reduced in numbers.

Whatever is projected by the collective consciousness of human-

ity—whether it is a vision of the Earth shifting its axis, a military con-
flagration, overpopulation, disease, drought, or famine—the collective
picture of the future of humanity is one of despair.

With this in mind, is there a way, a philosophy of life, or an ideol-
ogy that could replace despair with hope? Yes—and the example has
existed in our midst for thousands of years.

Adjacent to the industrial nations that suffer from the same syndrome exists another world—a world that is constantly shrinking. It
is the native world. In every part of the planet, native people are still
trying to claim their right to exist with philosophies and ways of life
that have been painstakingly developed to satisfy their "individual"
needs. The technical revolution has not been kind to them. In fact,
both physically and spiritually it has succeeded to a large degree in
annihilating them.

The world of native societies, once the rule, has now become the
exception. Strangely enough, however, these "primitive" societies are
those toward which the world of "big brother" is looking desperately
to find solutions to its own problems. And these are problems for
which natives have had solutions since time immemorial—solutions
that lie at the level of the subconscious, the intuitive, and the spiritual.

If a worldwide cataclysm were to occur, surviving native societies
would start over again just where they left off, with relatively little difficulty. For they know that the land is their sustenance—their mother,
as they call it—and that it could easily nurture them back to life. But
would there be a way for the technological world to reestablish its lost
balance? Would there be a way to recall wisdom and to supplant the
previously destructive behavior? It is doubtful.

As Teilhard de Chardin has pointed out, there exists in the consciousness of humanity a source of information that will never cease
to exist, if only humanity is willing to learn from it. The individual
most often relates to this source of information through prayer, meditation, contemplation—and, ultimately, revelation. By contrast, the
world of collectivism is constantly trying to dehumanize itself, forgetting the essential reasons for its existence.

"Man does not live by bread alone," we are told. By the same
token, the conveniences of a technological society will not counter-
balance the instability that the modern world has created in its own

consciousness. Modern society is seriously disturbed emotionally, and it needs immediate attention.

One hundred years is not enough time to make the emotional adjustment from horse-and-buggy days to the age of the space shuttle. Humanity's psyche is confused; it needs more time. Cellular evolution takes aeons. Rushing it has resulted only in confusion. The individual will eventually pull through, but collectively we will not—unless the trend to "collectivize" is reversed.

Although prevalent for more than a century, the classical theory of evolution first introduced by Charles Darwin is now challenged even by some in the scientific community, not to mention those in the religious community. Confused as to when and how Homo sapiens came into the world, many theories suggest that the composite personality of the human being (still connected to the animal kingdom and yet related to the angels) is a difficult combination to understand.

At any rate, we are forced to accept the fact that the key to understanding humanity's presence on Earth lies not with its collective accomplishments but with the individual. Even the "family," the smallest and most important of collective bodies, is geared to produce individuals, not institutions.

In the end, as it came to me in one of my reflections, the explanation for the human experience is the same as it always has been: ". . . a learning experience for the individual psyche, spirit, or soul, permitting it to refine itself by meeting the exigencies of each experience—*no matter what that experience might be*—with the total sum of abilities that each individual possesses."

Approaching this from a Christian standpoint, we could say that the distance each of us carries our cross is determined by the strength with which we are provided. This, in essence, constitutes our "human rights." Although somewhat obtuse and esoteric, this formula is the one that regulates our lives.

However, one question still remains to be answered. And that is, how can we efficiently transfer the colossal power acquired through the centuries by collective and institutionalized entities back to the individual?

First of all, today's society somehow must be convinced of the importance of individual expression—and truly believe that it is the only alternative to a holocaust. Eventually, modern telecommunications might be put to good use in spreading this truth beyond political and economic boundaries. The result might be the reintroduction into the psyche of humanity of a new hope for a balanced and more reasonable society—a hope that might replace our present feelings of fear, doom, and despair.

Life is a precious gift and must not be taken lightly. From the bowels of the Earth to the infinity of all universes, the chips are the same. In a multitude of alternatives, there is really only one choice: namely, to use the steeplechase of birth and death to win the Olympics of eternity in the best way possible. For the judge knows that a gold medal is won with each small effort along the way.

In writing this conclusion to *The Return of Pahana*, I have hoped not only to emphasize that now is the time for humanity to regain control of its destiny, but also to give some clues as to how we can go about doing that. I also have wanted to emphasize that hopes for social justice, although completely justified, are in the end only vain imaginings. That is not to say justice and equality do not exist; it is just that they do not exist as we would like to see them. Justice and equality exist not in legal or social terms, but only in the eyes of creation. All of us are created equal in our ability to deal with the challenges of our own individual lives. This is how human rights must be measured—not by any human yardstick but by the yardstick of spiritual justice that offers everyone a unique opportunity to expand spiritually through the joys and sorrows of living.

In light of this thought, street people, the homeless, the underprivileged, the sick, and the lame all have an equal chance to win a front-row seat in the theater of eternal life, right alongside the rich and the powerful. In the end, death and justice will admit everyone—not according to wealth or power, but according to the efforts each person has taken to remain pure, charitable, compassionate, and loving, regardless of the handicaps to which he or she has been submitted.

And now to the messages themselves . . .

PLACE OF PEACE

There is a place within each one of us where there is no hunger, no envy, no success or failure. As there is no limitation within that place, there is also peace. We are neither born to that place, nor do we die in it. It is permanent, and the only reality is that permanence. To get there, we must have only the willingness to think in terms of being there. This place has no name, no religion, no political affiliation. And when we are there, we think in the same terms as the next person who is there—creed, race, and color make no difference.

We don't go in or out of this place, as we take it with us. It is with us when we work, when we love, when we travel, when we eat or sleep. The place has no name, but the ones who are there know where and what it is.

This place is the only home we will ever know. When we are there, its warmth and peace fulfill in us the inner assurance we all have that somehow, somewhere we will find a world of endless contentment. Beyond birth, beyond death, beyond hunger and poverty, this place is the only reality—because when we get there, it never ends. Any other so-called "reality of life" is only illusion because it is only temporary.

After we arrive at the place of peace, the external expressions of everyday living, no matter what we may be involved in at the time, do not matter. Instead of struggling with the details of life in order to get ahead, we are now standing at the center of things. In "not wanting," we become part of the process of creation itself. This is a process in which the timing is not our own but is unbound by the limits of a day's work—or for that matter, an entire life's work. Our life is now a part of the whole, and our decisions are reflections of the great calendar of the cycles that has made life pulse from the very beginning. In "not acting," we become the greatest actors of all.

Is this passive resistance?. . . No.

Is this active nonviolence?. . . Perhaps.

What I *am* sure of is that as long as we remain in this place, we are a part of the Great Will. In so being, no fears, no pain, no negative thoughts or influences can reach us.

When we attain this place, perhaps in a small way we have reached a point in our spiritual evolution where we are part of the process of life itself—where, without remorse, impatience, hesitation, or blame, we experience only great compensation and great compassion.

THE ULTIMATE QUESTION

When will we have the opportunity to find out "what" we are?

Most of our lives, it seems, the only thing we know about ourselves is that we are an accumulation of the reflections of others. As children, we know what we are in comparison to mother, father, sisters, brothers, grandmother, and so on. And later on we define ourselves in relation to friends, teachers, lovers, and others.

What we know about ourselves, then, becomes a mosaic of impressions derived from being exposed to others. We entertain a myriad of sparkling thoughts about ourselves: that we are liked or disliked, tolerated or abused. And so we learn to evaluate ourselves in the flimsy light of these dancing electrodes without ever stopping to reflect about what it is that produces them.

Much later, perhaps when it does not matter anymore what others think, we finally ask ourselves the great question: What am I . . . *really?* Then we discover that we are not what other people saw in us at all or wanted us to be. We are original spirit entities that came into this world and then forgot our divinity. We are babes in an image of pain, seismic eruptions of blood and tears. And with our own blood and tears came our forgetfulness, as well as the chance to remember again.

OF TIME & HAPPINESS

Happiness is deeply linked to a sense of "permanence." It is not just a feeling but a state of being independent of time. Happiness depends on permanence, and on permanence alone.

To be thoroughly happy is to be content with what we are or are not, have or do not have. It is to be content to have what we need without wanting more. This is permanence indeed.

A mere state of euphoria is not happiness, as euphoria is merely the other side of depression. In order to strive toward a state of happiness, the span of a single life is not enough; the time is too short. Even to take refuge in the life of a nation or the slow march of an entire culture would not be enough time to find happiness. Against the spectrum of eternity, even the longest of human endeavors is but the blink of an eye. The life of humanity itself would be better, although still short.

No, happiness must be measured on the endless scale of life itself. In that light alone does our conscious and subconscious existence take on a meaning that nothing can disturb. In that light, wants and needs become one. Only when our wants and needs are one can we measure the depth and breadth of happiness without the limitations of time.

DIVINE WILL

The gate through which we pass to enter into a superior consciousness is characterized by the surrender of our personal will to a superior will: the Divine Will.

"Not mine, but thy will be done." Many have heard this phrase, but few have understood it. Fewer still have mastered it. But it is the key to any real advancement into the kingdom.

Our personal wills are limited first by our own lives and second by our physical bodies. Surrendering our wills to the Supreme Will, which has supported life in the universe throughout eternity, allows us to willingly incorporate our personal wills into the very mystery of creation.

To bring power into our lives, we must realize that it is first necessary to surrender to a power greater than ourselves. Who would willingly choose to cling to the tiny power of the individual when offered a partnership with the infinite Divine Will?

"Not mine, but thy will be done." This is the key, not only to spiritual survival, but also to peace within—and therefore to happiness on Earth for all people of goodwill.

EARTH SCHOOL

"History repeats itself." We hear this comment often in the course of our lives. Put another way, it might be stated, "People never learn." Yet nothing could be more inaccurate or more indicative of a total misunderstanding of humanity's purpose on this planet.

Planet Earth is a huge schoolhouse. Classes follow classes as they do yearly in any schoolhouse. And in the short run, at least, the benefit does not go to the institution but to the pupils.

History is also part of the schoolhouse, and the individuals who have "passed through" are the ones who have benefited from the learning experience. They have inscribed on their souls, spirits, or psyches—however one wishes to express it—the passage from one life to another, the process of death and rebirth.

Within the schoolhouse of Planet Earth, all students must take certain subjects in order to present themselves for the final exam at the end of the "school year." As in any school curriculum, some subjects are very basic. And despite all the recording devices humanity has invented through the ages (language, books, records, tapes, computers, films, televison, etc.), these basic subjects have not appreciably changed through the ages.

Humanity must still learn the basics. On the one hand, there are courses in inhumanity, deprivation, injustice, hunger, catastrophe, and war. But these courses are primarily to help us learn the far more important lessons of love, peace, joy, compassion, and understanding. These are all part of the standard curriculum.

Of course, some students do not pass the grade and have to repeat. These are the students who may benefit most from the experience of reincarnation.

The statement "People never learn," then, is a misjudgment of the whole process of human life—a misinterpretation resulting from an ignorance of the fact that we all go from class to class using the revolving door of birth and death.

In the end, the final "degree" we are awarded proves that we do learn—eventually. And then we do not have to come back to school again. The institution, however, while upgrading its curriculum from time to time, stays basically the same.

"IN THY NAME"

There is so much being done "in thy name"!

Different names for and ways of looking at God are really only different ways of worshiping the same deity. Different religions, churches, and cults are only different ways of viewing reality and the world. Yet "in thy name," people kill each other, simply because of the different angles from which they view the same God.

Why have we not discovered that forms are of no great importance but merely different vehicles to reach the same end? Some like it slow, some like it fast; some like it silent, some like it loud. Some even like to shout Thy Name as if everyone else were deaf. Some like to worship through dancing, singing, and drumming; some are quiet, some ebullient.

Some call Thy Name "creative energy"; some call it "Divine Will." The American Indian made obeisance to the "Great Spirit." But what difference does it all make, so long as we know we are a part of it, a part of the All, a part of Thy Name?

To be part of something means that we care about it; if we didn't, we would be part of something else. Would we be with the kachinas who dance all night long, punctuated by the rhythm of drums in the kivas? Would we be in a great cathedral, or within the decrees of the Vatican, or in the golden temples of India or Mecca? Rest assured, these are all simply the ways of humanity, the many alleys devised to reach the true meaning of Thy Name.

In two thousand years someone will still say, "What have we learned? Who are we? Aren't we the ones—the great, great, great grandchildren of the ones—who saw Abraham, Moses, Christ, Buddha, and Mohammed?"

As the multitudes once said of Christ, "Kill him, kill him!"—he who had done nothing but love them—so today the multitudes still cry out to kill the spiritual leaders who love them. But are these the same multitudes who refused the first time?

Children of humanity, may you learn that love, and love alone, is the eternal way that fixes the stars in the heavens, attracts the atoms of the Earth to one another, and holds mothers in adoration of the little ones in their arms.

The great Teacher of them all has no name, and knows that it will always be so.

UNITY

The mountain climber knows as he climbs the frozen wastes of the high altitudes that he has yet to discover the immensities that lie beyond the peaks he is climbing. So, too, the deep-sea diver knows as he puts on his wet suit, armor of the deep, and goes down many fathoms that the sea is in no way what the sailor or the swimmer sees on the surface. The greater immensity is below.

And so it is for the spiritual climber progressing toward that place often written about—the place that encompasses all horizons, all colors of the spiritual prism, all places both far and deep. From there, the immensity and depths are no longer hidden from view. Gradually, by the light of the rising central sun, we see the distant peaks, the undersea chasms. We know their names, heights, and locations.

Forever after we will know that these things are not hidden but part of the immensity of all experience. United with every corner and portion of the whole, we see all, nothing apart. What we have discovered is unity—alike and different, known and unknown, light and dark, forever the totality, never to be forgotten. We are now a part of it, co-creators with spirit for all time to come.

SURRENDER

It is difficult for human actions, all of which depend on will to some extent, to incorporate the spectrum of life as a whole and as a process. Still, only with this "total" view are we insured that we can immerse the self into the primary dimensions we have to work with on Planet Earth—namely, those of time and space.

No matter how clever, cunning, or technically advanced humanity becomes, however, its egocentric acts will not bring it into time and space in such a way that it shares the experience of perfect harmony with all other planes of reality. Only one attitude guarantees that a humanly conceived action will be a part of the process of creation itself: an attitude of surrender to the "universal will."

Surrender to Divine Will is not fatalism. Surrender is a positive and perfectly conscious action conceived and executed with the knowledge that we can incorporate our own personal energies into a greater form of energy—a supreme form of energy, in fact—which is the Supreme Intelligence that regulates all there is.

Surrender is not negation, either; quite the opposite, it is the affirmation of our desire to become nothing in order to become part of everything. The subsequent view that we have of place and order in things becomes that of the spiritual mountain climber or deep-sea diver: a glimpse of the complete and beautiful world of the heights and the depths.

The grain of wheat that helps make the dough in the leavened loaf of bread—is it not part of the loaf? In its own infinitesimal way, it *is* the loaf. So each grain of sand, without which there would be no beach, becomes the beach itself.

And the human will, deciding to surrender to the global intelligence that is life, becomes part of the total will, an intelligent co-creator knowing full well the meaning of each action on the beaches of time.

THE PRESENT MOMENT

Consciously or unconsciously, everyone dreams of doing what is right. Although human morals are quite different from universal ones, if someone does something "right," he or she must be doing it in "unison"—or rather, in the time and space that is universal—because this is what makes it "right." Then the act itself becomes a child of that moment in time, that speck of eternity in which nothing is really right or wrong but simply *is.*

If we are concerned only with the "now," we are working on a level of consciousness so restricted that anything can change our course—just as a feather dropped from a second-story window would be affected by any air current that comes along. However, if we place ourselves in such a dimension that whatever we do will be of equal value whether seen from yesterday's or tomorrow's point of view, then what we have done will stand the test of time. In so acting, we have entered the dimension of permanence.

In order to enter this space, it is futile to want to do things *our way*; rather, we must think in terms of action for the sake of time itself, time being the test of whether our actions are true. In doing so, we give up our individual will for the will of time, which, in its ongoingness contains a far greater truth than our individual wills.

It is not easy to find the unique moment that will make any action true. Doing so requires lifting ourselves above the nitty-gritty of the everyday grindstone so that we can discover inside us the common denominator that always exists between ourselves and the essence of time.

Then, if what happens as a result of our actions is in accordance with what we wanted to happen, fine. But if it is not, that is also fine, because what we really wanted was to place ourselves in the eternal moment, the "is." In the end, doing so is what will make us truly real, truly happy, and at peace with ourselves and the world.

PATIENCE

It is sad to watch people and the society they belong to hurry along toward their deaths. One might expect that humanity would take its time. But no, the human race (with the exception of what is left of the primal world) hurries to everything, including its own funeral. The mass of humanity is exceedingly impatient.

Impatience is not only a sign of immaturity, a remnant of childhood, but it also runs counter to the proper values of time; it falsifies time. A bigger net catches more fish than a small one. Likewise, patience catches more time than impatience. And in doing so it gives us a greater opportunity to find out just what we are doing on Earth at this moment in time. Once we know this, we will be better able to answer the crucial question of *how* we are going to accomplish what we are doing—and where and when—which is the formula for happiness.

In other words, a hurried mode of life, both individually and collectively, forbids us to enter the true fabric of life. Only time and patience allow this to happen.

It does not take much knowledge of human psychology to understand that crowding too many things into a day shortens the day. On the other hand, if we allow time to create "space" in our lives, we will have more freedom to choose—and to introduce reflection into a world that seems bent on driving itself crazy. In concert with time is timelessness. In harmony with timelessness is deathlessness. There is no hurry in rushing to that which is never going to happen.

PLENTY

In an age in which people are taught to create more and more needs for themselves, it is good to meditate on the essence of plenty.

Like mountain climbers who see all from the summit and have no desire to see more, so spiritual climbers have no desire to see more than what is available to them at the time of their ascension. They are perfectly satisfied with what they get in the moment.

The essence of plenty centers on the needs of the seeker and not with his or her wishes or desires. Needs are controlled by the fact that too much is too much; wishes and desires cannot be controlled, as enough is never enough.

HOME

To emerge, to see, to find our individual place in the order of things, we must rise out of ourselves in total nakedness. Like the pulp of a fruit, the grain of wheat, or the kernel of corn that sparkles after being peeled, so must we be pressed between the divine fingers of the Creator—the essence of the self finally cleansed of its prison cell, naked and free, unencumbered at last.

Just as the new babe instantly becomes a member of the community it was born into, so we all emerge in the pattern of things aware, finally, that peace is not what we know of ourselves, or within our house, or surrounding our family, but everywhere. Home, when found, brings true recognition and peace.

WHY?

People take the elevator to go to the top of the Mark Hopkins, the Empire State Building, the Eiffel Tower, happy to see the far-reaching view beyond the big city. They build huge cranes to lift monstrous weights, subterranean trains to fly underground, and all manner of fancy conveyances. However, people don't think of descending into their own depths or speeding out of their own self-centered thoughts in order to see the outer limits of creation, as near to them as their own noses.

Weightlessness, the speed of light, everywhere and always—dimensions and domains far greater than the circumferences of great cities—are available to us all. Still, many will not lift a finger to travel out of their self-imposed limits.

Why?

SEX

Sex is not present one moment and gone the next. Sex is everywhere in nature, at all times.

Sex is electricity. Sex is biodynamics. Sex is electromagnetism. Sex is chemistry and astrology.

Sex is neither good nor bad.

Polarity and expansion are sexual laws that need not be explained; they are self-evident. Poles attract each other. Stars, planets, and galaxies that are well balanced in space are energized to stay that way — through sex.

In our lack of wisdom, we have separated what has been united, misused what has been given for our use, forgotten what has been given for our gain.

MEANING

The way to discover the meaning of our lives is to take them out of context. Being too close to anything distorts the overall picture in which meaning is to be found.

One way to take our lives out of context is to place ourselves apart from them. For example, what would we see if we observed a colony of ants in an anthill? If we looked too closely, we would not be able to detect, from the life of one particular ant, what the purpose of the whole community was about. But if we sat back and gazed at the whole colony for a while, we would see it without a doubt. The distance from our eyes to the myriad of ants, following each other in endless procession, would provide a good picture of the meaning of the lives of ants: protection of the species.

So it is when we take "a back seat" and observe the process of our own lives—observe them as parts of the larger life around them. Only then do we discover the direction in which the All goes—and therefore the direction of our individual lives. We no longer focus on the extraneous and the transient, but on the whole that includes them. We see then the endless procession of human will incorporated into the greater will, the Divine Will, without which no other will can exist.

REVELATION

An abstract picture, a nonrepresentative painting, makes sense only when the separate details are studied and brought into harmony with one another. In such a way the mind becomes slowly readied to understand the whole, the sum of the parts.

Similarly, revelation occurs after the spirit has been adequately prepared to receive the ultimate lesson. After long preparation, which conditions the recipient for the gift of wisdom, it descends quite naturally.

Shortcuts to wisdom only diminish its value, for the time of receiving is not the time of wanting but the time in which the gift is naturally born, its own time—thus, when it can best be received.

BEYOND POSITIVE & NEGATIVE

Since God is positive energy, the only real sin is negativity.

Just as individual thought can be positive or negative, so can the collective thought of humanity. Murder, rape, theft, and the like are negative individual expressions of our collective consciousness, just as hope, kindness, and compassion are positive expressions of the collective mind.

The qualities inherent in our individual wills predispose us either to positivity, negativity, or both—for the face of our world appears to be polarized. Truth is ultimately positive, and positive energy will inevitably triumph even on Earth; however, as human beings our ultimate reality will be governed primarily by one or the other of these polarized creative forces.

Positive and negative: may the difference between the two not separate but unite. May the difference between the two become the unity that transcends both—the radiant path to the light that leaves behind the murky waters of hesitation, compromise, corruption, and sin.

POWER

It is through our love for God that God shares universal power with us. The more intense our love, the greater the power.

Just as we turn our faces toward the sun, the greater power, in a similar manner we can turn toward God to share divine radiance and power.

However, just as the sun brings solace, it can also burn.

We must, therefore, be prepared to handle power as it comes to us—freely, bountifully, and with love. Misused, power destroys; used with care and consideration (as it was intended), it can bring only goodness.

So can we all be co-creators of a world that knows no end, no boundaries—a world expanding *ad vitam eternam*.

ESSENCE & THE SPIRAL

The point of contact, the connecting link, that unites people of all creeds and colors is "essence." Essence is the extract of life that binds us all to the reasons for which we were dispatched to this world. And despite the ideological and cultural differences dividing humanity against itself, a constant vision of the essence in all things can bind us together instead of pulling us apart.

The spiral is the symbol of all essences. Following the direction indicated by this spiritual symbol of all beginnings, we can find communion with each other as brothers and sisters "in essence."

Though the spiral is composed of multiple concentric circles moving outward and upward, all of the circles begin at the same single point: the point of creation. Just so, in spite of our divergent beliefs and backgrounds, we can remember the spiral and prepare ourselves to go back to a system of life in which the all and the many are one.

BIRTH

When a new babe comes into the world, where that babe is born is not as important as the reason for which it came. However, as the babe grows more aware of its surroundings, environmental pressures come to bear. Soon the child will forget the real reason for its coming in favor of conditioning to the society of which it is a member.

What a pity, for none of the cultural elements surrounding the child are essential or even important. In fact, most of the proud accomplishments of humanity are unimportant next to the reasons for individual births.

If culture, society, and civilization were of paramount importance to us, then it stands to reason that we would be allowed to take at least some of it with us when we die. But we cannot! What good is it to us—all that costly cultural claptrap—when none of it can be retained?

Whether born into riches or poverty, whether taught to respect or deny God, whether conservative or progressive, communist or capitalist, none of this can we take with us when our time comes to "go home." Cultures, ideologies, skin colors, religious or geographical boundaries—none is essential.

Looking at the history of humanity, it might seem that there is a progression, a development, or an evolution that has taken place throughout time—an evolution through which hundreds of billions of individual souls have come to bear earthly witness.

But all of this is an illusion. If we look closely at the birth-life-death process, underneath the varnish of so-called evolution characterized by cultural, social, and religious developments, Homo sapiens has not changed. Humanity is just as violent, forgetful, and egocentric as ever. The methods for killing, impressing, and deceiving are more sophisticated, perhaps, but that is all. Humanity, originally born in innocence and truth, still learns how to avoid its purpose, its birthright.

On the other hand, regardless of differences in character, each individual born into a particular period of history learns what he or she needs to learn from it. We should give less emphasis to the form and more to the process of life.

When we are first born—whether we are children of the rich or poor, capitalist or communist, Gentile or Jew—we could care less about the conditions in which we find ourselves. What is paramount for us as individuals is what we *make* of our backgrounds, regardless of what they might be.

FRIENDSHIP

It is often difficult for us to relate to our fellow humans with compassion and love, as one spirit to another. That is because, tricked and temporarily blinded by our condition, we look solely at the differences in each other. This blinds us to our common brotherhood.

Deep within ourselves we could recapture the reality of our lives if we would only look at each other as fellow travelers, the repositories of universal spirit and energy. Knowing this to be true, we might then recognize and remember each other. And this memory of our true status might help us to understand that what separates us is only false and temporary.

With the intimate knowledge that our real and permanent home is not here on Earth, we could then sympathize with and befriend each other.

We need to recognize what we really are: spirits entrapped in physical bodies. This is a condition we have all accepted in order to learn more about life. When we know from deep within that there are no differences, then we can experience the simple but profound quality that philosophers and poets, saints and visionaries have been speaking of through the ages: friendship.

PERSPECTIVE

The true greatness of a culture is to be measured not by its physical accomplishments, but by the spiritual growth of its people. Out of the dusts of past civilizations, the way is still unclear. The riddle of existence is still our very reason for being. We live in order to more fully understand who we are.

With most animals, the role of the individual seems clear. With man, who has left the Garden of Eden, freedom of choice has led to the creation of sophisticated intellectual structures, including cultures and civilizations. And with these have come endless and complicated screens to be placed between Creator and creation.

As Jesus once said, let us give back to Caesar what belongs to Caesar and to God what belongs to God. Cultures, societies, and religions all have their place in our learning program, but only if we recognize them for what they are: not the curriculum itself, but only the tools by which to comprehend it.

Though we are all physical beings, let us not forget that the purpose of our presence on Earth is solely to give spirit a chance to record experience—nothing else. Let us give back to Caesar the trimmings and keep the essence with us forever.

WAR & PEACE, BODY & SPIRIT

War and peace are but two edges of the same sword—a sword that fashions our lives on Earth to such an extent that our very existence depends on it.

We live at all times in a world at war, a world in conflict. Volcanic eruptions, earthquakes, cancer, heart disease, traffic fatalities, alcoholism, drugs, famine—there is no end to the struggle and danger.

Our greatest epics have been inspired by raging oceans, stormy skies, and brutal battlefields. Life itself is a battlefield. Peace is balance and harmony, not stagnation and fossilization. Fires, floods, avalanches, pestilence, and war are the components of war and peace. They are the price we pay for a cosmic balance that hinges far beyond the boundaries of a single lifetime.

As the lives of Christ, Buddha, and Gandhi so plainly demonstrate, dangers to the body can mean the salvation of the soul. On the other hand, prostitution of the body can mean the death of the soul—the soul that survives fire, flood, and war.

Shall we weep for the loss of a body that began to die the day it was born? Or shall we weep for the death of a spirit that was born so long ago no scientist can say when it began?

FREEDOM

Freedom is the opportunity to utilize our environment to best advantage in order to learn.

Rich, poor, healthy, or sick—all are equal states in which to learn, expand, and progress. If it were not so, then the human experience, with all its inequalities and injustices, would have no meaning.

The important thing, then, is to pay attention to the opportunities provided by our individual condition. In this singular realization, freedom becomes our own.

CHRIST

Giant among giants, Christ came to give humanity the key to its very existence. To contemplate what we know of Christ's life—his birth in most miserable conditions, his death on the gallows of his day, and his ultimate resurrection—gives us the key to understanding the presence of humanity on Earth.

Here was a temporary presence with a beginning and an end, just like our own, characterized by the bold simplicity of ultimate nakedness. Yet for his wisdom and suffering, he was given the seal of redemption through resurrection of body and spirit.

Standing as an obelisk, a beacon of humanity, Christ made it possible to understand the role of suffering as the indispensable process through which individualized spirit must pass in order to understand itself.

History without Christ would be like life without oxygen. His birth, life, and death serve as a catalyst that can keep our own lives in focus.

THE IMMACULATE

The "immaculate" is a dimension, not a state. It is the nothingness. It is the void that preceded form and matter. It is that which came before the world of ordered creation.

The word "immaculate" usually conjures images of pure white, yet white is the only color that is not a color; it is all colors. Immaculateness is not a quality, characteristic, or status—it preceded all that.

Before the matter of creation even existed, the spirit form was in slow motion; the nothing was spotless, faultless, and formless.

"I am the Immaculate," Mary said to Bernadette. By this Mary meant that she was the one who preceded all the rest, the one who gave meaning to everything that came after.

THE STAGE & THE PLAY OF LIFE

No matter how richly decorated is the stage of a theater before a performance, it becomes meaningful only when a performer appears. The stage was conceived for that purpose. No one would mistake the stage for the performer, yet the two go inextricably together. The stage was meant to support the performer.

This is also true in the broader play of human life. Civilization's sole purpose is to serve as the vehicle, the decor—the stage, if you will—for the performance of individual lives. It was meant as the foundation, the setting, for individual men, women, and children to perform the ritual of earthly life.

Like stages, institutions may change, but the ritual remains the same.

THE EARTH

The Earth is that special place where individual spirit matter is "conceptualized." Like medication put into capsules in an industrialized plant, the human experiment is the plant that helps conceptualize the individual spirit.

Trapped in the human body for the duration of a lifetime, the spirit is released at the end of the journey more refined, more aware, one step closer to being reunited forever with the "matrix" that once conceived it.

THE VESSEL

Because of the very nature of the senses that have been given to us for the experience of physical incarnation, it is extremely difficult for us to maintain a realistic view of ourselves.

Seeing, hearing, feeling, tasting, and touching all convey the impression that physical sensation is paramount and possibly the sole reason for our being here.

However, with a sharpened awareness, it is possible to sense more than we thought possible. For instance, it is known that wine appears to taste better when presented in a rich decanter or a bottle with a well-known label. Similarly, a trip in a Rolls Royce or a Cadillac might give more pleasant impressions than the same trip taken in an old truck. But these sensations are projections of the mind triggered by the nature of the "vehicle," or "vessel."

The same process affects our minds when we think of ourselves as sensory beings. Projection leads to the conviction that our physical condition is indeed paramount, but this is only an illusion. A primitive human looking down from the top of a mountain after a hunt must have had a much different view of himself than a New Yorker looking down from the Empire State Building—not just because their environments are so different, but also because the processes that each uses to view his or her life are so different.

We have a tendency to think that the vessel is all we are—that this "vehicle" that transports us from birth to death is paramount. We forget that what we really are is a bit of heaven on Earth.

A few years ago our physical bodies were not even here; in another few years they will be gone, forced as we are to leave them when our human experiment comes to an end. This should help us to keep the proper perspective on birth and death, and to realize that the vehicle is not the experience itself.

Judeo-Christian beliefs have apparently not made this very clear, though the distinction has been recorded in the sacred texts. But somehow it did not register well enough; otherwise, we modern humans would not be so materialistic.

Our techno-industrial society needs a new approach to understanding life—an approach that is relative rather than absolute, humble and searching rather than so arrogant and cocksure. And that approach needs to go beyond the physical senses in order to comprehend a wider reality.

HISTORY & THE INDIVIDUAL

Contrary to historical belief, all of the interactions and experiences that justify political, social, economic, or religious institutions are, in fact, strictly for the purpose of educating the human soul, that speck of universal spirit that is locked within each one of us. Only when we realize that direction and purpose are individual, not collective, will history finally fit into its proper perspective. Only then will it be freed of the self-centeredness that cultures, societies, and civilizations have injected into it. No matter what happens then, history will be seen in its true light.

Similarly, the highest morality is not devotion to a particular society or religion, but an unconditional love for the human condition. This love in itself leads us automatically to love our neighbor and, ultimately, to love the creative principle from which we have come.

THE DIVINE PLAN

Ultimate morality has appeared repeatedly on the screen of humanity in order to protect the original plan designed for us aeons ago.

This original plan is now being threatened by the imperfection of human thought, resulting in the destruction of both our environment and many of our individual lives. However, through a principle of constant rejuvenation, the "plot" remains ever the same. The Earth, which is itself a living being, balances humankind's deficiencies with reactions of its own. In other words, no one can put asunder what the Divine Will has put together.

The enlightened souls who pave the way as the plot develops show us that we must have patience, faith, and trust in the way to come. While humanity as a whole will vacillate between love and fear, joy and despair, our responsibility as individuals is to realize our souls through our Earth experience and to know that the plan will continue undisturbed.

In this process, death is the revolving door to life, the ultimate experience that each soul has to face. Without it, it would not be possible to check on the progress made by the soul. And the timing of death is relevant to the soul itself—not to the attachments the soul has made in its short passage on Earth.

EVOLUTION

The human experience is not really a continuum that leads to higher and more sophisticated societies and cultures, but rather an educational system for the individual that becomes more elaborate and challenging as the individual progresses through successive lives. This is due to the fact that through the reincarnation of the human soul, higher levels of spiritual awareness, or "educational tools," are required for the self-realization of spirit matter.

This realization gives a much better understanding of humanity's evolutional processes than that of the scientific community—which, by the way, has never been able to agree on what principle evolution is based.

BODY & SPIRIT

The personalization of global spirit matter that becomes the individual soul occurs on the level of form: the physical body. That is to say, that portion of the global spirit that enters the individual at birth is shaped by the person who houses it during the earthly experience.

It is logical and reasonable to say that the soul retains the characteristics of the human aura as it perfects itself through subsequent incarnations. This is necessary for its refinement and self-realization, which is the primary purpose of the human experience. As the process follows the intricacies of time, the global universal spirit evolves a little at a time, giving the universe the chance to "know" itself.

Thus, we have a system through which each particle becomes a person before entering the universal system itself.

INJUSTICE & EXPERIENCE

Contradictory though it may seem, social injustice in human life is a necessity. Not only does it provide critical experience for the soul, but it creates the climate of opposites that leads to ultimate balance.

Every man, woman, and child should have enough to eat and a roof over their heads. Since many do not, the human need for social justice stirs up a great deal of controversy—and a great deal of spiritual growth.

But let us not forget that the chief need of humanity is not justice but *experience*—experience that will school the soul on its journey to ultimate realization. If we could magically do away with all injustice, we would deprive the soul of its full range of experience, the very reason for human existence.

Of course, we must *not* encourage social injustice; after all, the struggle for justice is also an important part of the soul's experience. However, it is important for us to remember that injustice, like pain, suffering, and conflict of all kinds, is an important crucible for the soul. Out of conflict have been born the saints of the world, not to mention the great performers, explorers, philosophers, musicians, and scientists of all time.

Let us remember that peace is balance and moderation, not stagnation, fixation, and death.

INSTITUTION VERSUS INDIVIDUAL

In looking at the world today and trying to put it in perspective, it is clear that the political, religious, and social institutions that make up humanity's legacy on Earth are not viable entities unto themselves, but exist only for the benefit of humanity. Remove the individual, and the institution becomes nothing but an empty shell.

It is therefore clear that the only entities directly involved with the process of human life—the entities that justifiy the existence of the institution—are the men, women, and children who benefit from them. Human institutions are merely conveniences. They exist only as long as there is someone to use them; otherwise, they are nonexistent and useless.

This is important for us to remember as we move into the twenty-first century. For in recent times, governments, tribunals, offices, firms, agencies, and institutions of all kinds have become paramount unto themselves. Those who direct them have forgotten their original purpose: to serve individual human beings.

But the message goes deeper, too. Humanity, this aggregation of individual souls, is the carrier of the "spirit flame" for which all institutions are but the candle holders. In the years just ahead, institutions will be asked to shed the immense power they have acquired through the ages and to return it to the human beings they serve.

It is easy to understand why many governments, monarchs, and dictators have chosen to eliminate the individuals who have challenged or threatened their power. However, in doing so, the institutions have committed crimes against humanity. Human history confirms this. And today's history-in-the-making will confirm it.

THE GREAT PLAY OF LIFE

Actors play many roles, including scenes of war, murder, incest, rape, and other atrocities. Still, in the end, the play or film, as well as its actors, is transcended by the greater morality upon which the story is based. When each actor goes home, he or she thinks of the role that has been played only in light of the story of which it was a part.

And so with the human condition. The story was written long ago, once and for all. The roles remain constant; only the players and scenes change. As it is on stage, when the actors in human life "go home," they take with them only the memories of the spectacle—the reactions of the public, their visions of how their parts were played, and the morality or immorality of the acts of a particular day. When the play is over, only memory remains.

Thus, death is the real key to the understanding of life. Birth and death are intimately connected, one being the opposite side of the other. But only the implacable reality of death gives clear meaning to life—the play that repeats itself night after night, lifetime after lifetime.

SEXUALITY & SPIRITUALITY

Sexuality is the basic component that gives life the energy it needs to attain the goals set in motion by the process of creation.

Not to incorporate sexuality into the mainstream of spirituality is not only unnatural but opens the door to all sorts of abuse. Sexuality must be treated with consideration and respect, as it will not easily let itself be suppressed. Nor will it allow itself to be used solely for procreation or for selfish enjoyment.

Tibetan, Indian, Japanese, and Chinese tantric traditions utilize sexuality for spiritual growth and liberation. If not used in such a positive fashion, sexuality can be sadly repressed through excessive discipline and unrealistic moral standards or abused and turned into negative currents that lead eventually to crime and aberrations such as rape, incest, and child abuse.

Eroticism is an integral and healthy part of humanity's energy pattern. Philosophy, psychology, history, and even religion confirm it as a healthy, natural human preoccupation. The Eastern tantric practice of raising the kundalini energy has proven to be an efficient way of incorporating sexual energy into spiritual growth and liberation. We in the West, who so often seem mired in sexual hang-ups, would do well to study this practice.

HUMANITY & THE INDIVIDUAL

Humanity has grown greatly through the centuries, spreading first across the arable parts of the world and now seemingly into every nook and cranny imaginable. Now in great cities, individuals everywhere find themselves mere specks in a pernicious flood of human population.

Through the ages, population growth has produced a state of being in which individuals have lost some of their original significance—trading it for the power of the masses, the institutions, and the collective consciousness. This process has in turn produced a psychosis, a mass hysteria, in which human energy is mostly given to "Moloch," the aggregate of nations.

The first and most obvious result of this polarization of energy toward the collective is not solely that it detracts from the individual self, but that it has changed the way humanity *thinks* of itself. The fantastic growth and weight of modern society has affected the perception that humanity has of its own destiny.

Little by little, an "evolutionary vision" of humanity's works has developed through the centuries, gradually replacing the original perception of a personalized vision. Primitive humanity has never had such delusions. Primitive humanity has always understood the cyclic purpose of death and therefore not forgotten that its vision was individualistic in nature.

Material accomplishments, wealth, poverty, war, peace, health, or illness are not the issues of humanity; they are only the means to be used for personal growth. We are not permitted to keep our physical bodies as we go on toward our eternal destinies. Our bodies are merely the vehicles that permit us to cross the stage of human experience.

Similarly, the physical works that we have contributed— including monuments and even societies—ultimately have to be given up so that the stage upon which human destiny fulfills itself is not so crowded that a new individual cannot walk across it.

HUMANITY'S TRUE GOAL

We humans are well endowed with the ability to feel our environment through our sense of touch; to smell the odors of the world through our noses; to taste the flavors of foods with our tongues; to listen to the sounds of the day through our ears; and to see the shape and color of the world through the marvelous lens of the human eye. Yet our senses deceive us; the important thing is not *what* we sense but *why* we sense.

Modern humanity has spent most of its effort and energy creating material evidence for its own genius. Meanwhile, the spiritual foundation upon which everything else rests attracts but a trickle of interest. The very cause of the physical aspect of things is the spiritual foundation underlying and feeding it; humanity is the effect, not the cause.

Culture after culture has used the immense power of the human personality to build fleeting monuments to its passing. In so doing, humanity has largely bypassed the realities that could help it to understand and fulfill the very reason for its presence on planet Earth.

Culture after culture, each thinking itself the ultimate expression of the planetary will, has become mired in evolutionary projection, thereby missing the unique reason for the human experience—which depends on the connection of every individual to the spiritual source of existence.

The only real power humanity has is the power to realize for itself *why it is,* and that is all. Given this, our task is obvious: to rehumanize ourselves; to lead society back to its original and only goal. It is time for us all to find a way out of the dehumanizing mass consciousness and return to discover the beauty and timelessness of our true selves.

The preceding "messages" were recorded throughout 1983. For the next seven years, the author puzzled over their source. Finally, on a June morning in 1990, it became clear that the "messages" had been communicated by a very close friend of his, Edward O'Brien—a scholar, theologian, and renowned muralist—who had died in 1975. Before O'Brien's death, he and the author had had many discussions about the ideas that later appeared in the "messages," and their style strongly resembles O'Brien's own style of expression.

E N D N O T E S

---

1. *There are several so-called "Chief Seattle" addresses that are said to be original responses to President Pierce's offer to buy the Indians' land. One reason for this is that several different people recorded the chief's words on that day in 1854, and it is likely that the recordings differed somewhat because of language problems and interpretation. Another reason is that the chief himself was a very eloquent speaker, and it is likely that his words have been borrowed and amplified by various writers over the years.*

For example, though there are definitely elements of the chief's speech in the address printed here, it is probably inaccurate in many respects. Chief Seattle was a Salish Indian; it is unlikely that he had a great attachment to the plains, the buffalo, or the pinon pines. His was a land of forested inlets, beaches, salmon, and towering fir trees.

Yet "his" various speeches, whether accurate or not, live on and continue to be quoted again and again, mainly because they were all inspired by the sentiment and the beautiful spirit of the old chief himself.

With this in mind, I offer here two other renditions of the Chief Seattle Address. The first, recorded by H. Smith during the chief's actual appearance, is probably a more accurate rendition than the more poetic account in the Introduction. I also include Smith's description of the old man and the scene, as it helps to bring the speaker alive and to authenticate the account.

Old Chief Seattle was the largest Indian I ever saw, and by far the noblest looking. He stood nearly six feet in his moccasins, was broad shouldered, deep chested and finely proportioned. His eyes were large, intelligent, expressive and friendly when in repose, and faithfully mirrored the varying moods of the great soul that looked through them. He was usually solemn, silent and dignified, but on great occasions he moved among assembled multitudes like a Titan among Lilliputians, and his lightest word was law.

When rising to speak in council or to tender advice, all eyes were turned upon him, and deep-toned, sonorous and eloquent sentences rolled from his lips like the ceaseless thunders of cataracts flowing from exhaustless fountains, and his magnificent bearing was as noble as that of the most cultivated military chieftain in command of the forces of a continent. Neither his eloquence, his dignity or his grace was acquired. They were as native to his manhood as leaves and blossoms are to a flowering almond.

His influence was marvellous. He might have been an emperor but all his instincts were democratic, and he ruled his loyal subjects with kindness and paternal dignity. He was always flattered by marked attention from white men, and never so much as when seated at their tables, and on such occasions he manifested more than anywhere else the genuine instincts of a gentleman.

When Governor Stevens first arrived in Seattle and told the natives that he had been appointed Commissioner of Indian Affairs for Washington Territory, they gave him a demonstrative reception in front of Dr. Maynard's office, near the water front on Main Street. The Bay swarmed with canoes and the shore was lined with a living mass of swaying, writhing, dusky humanity, until old Chief Seattle's trumpet-toned voice rolled over the immense multitude, like the startling reveille of a bass drum, when silence became as instantaneous and perfect as that which follows a clap of thunder from a clear sky.

The Governor was then introduced to the native multitude by Dr. Maynard, and at once commenced, in a conversational, plain and straightforward style, an explanation of his mission among them, which is too well understood to require recapitulation.

When he sat down, Chief Seattle arose, with all the dignity of a senator who carries the responsibilities of a great nation on his shoulders. Placing one hand on the Governor's head, and slowly pointing heavenward with the index finger of the other, he commenced his memorable address in solemn and impressive tones:

"Yonder sky has wept tears of compassion on our fathers for centuries untold, and that which to us looks eternal, may change. Today it is fair, tomorrow it may be overcast with clouds. My words are like the stars that never set. What Seattle says the great chief [in] Washington can rely upon, with as much certainty as our pale-face brothers can rely upon the return of the seasons.

"The son of the white chief says his father sends us greetings of friendship and goodwill. This is kind, for we know he has little need of our friendship in return, because his people are many. They are like the grass that covers the vast prairies, while my people are few, and resemble the scattering trees of a windswept plain.

"The great, and I presume also good, white chief sends us word that he wants to buy our lands but is willing to allow us to reserve enough to live on comfortably. This indeed appears generous, for the red man no longer has rights that he need respect, and the offer may be wise, also, for we are no longer in need of a great country. There was a time when our people covered the whole land as the waves of a wind-ruffled sea cover its shell-paved floor. But that time has long since passed away with the greatness of tribes almost forgotten. I will not mourn over our untimely decay, nor reproach my pale-face brothers with hastening it, for we, too, may have been somewhat to blame.

"When our young men grow angry at some real or imaginary wrong and disfigure their faces with black paint, their hearts also are disfigured and turn black, and then their cruelty is relentless and knows no bounds, and our old men are not able to restrain them. But let us hope that hostilities between the red man and his pale-face brothers may never return. We would have everything to lose and nothing to gain. True it is that revenge, with our young braves, is considered gain, even at the cost of their own lives, but old men who stay at home in times of war, and old women who have sons to lose, know better.

"Our great father [in] Washington, for I presume he is now our father as well as yours . . . sends us word by his son, who, no doubt, is a great chief among his people, that if we do as he desires, he will protect us. His brave armies will be to us a bristling wall of strength, and his great ships of war will fill our harbors so that our ancient enemies far to the north-ward, the Simsiams and Hydas, will no longer frighten our women and old men. Then he will be our father and we will be his children.

"But can this ever be? Your God loves your people and hates mine; he folds his strong arms lovingly around the white man and leads him as a father leads his infant son, but he has forsaken his red children. He makes your people wax strong every day, and soon they will fill the land; while our people are ebbing away like a fast-receding tide that will never flow again. The white man's God cannot love his red children or he would protect them. They seem to be orphans and can look nowhere for help. How then can we become brothers? How can your father become our father and bring us prosperity and awaken in us dreams of returning greatness?

"Your God seems to be partial. He came to the white man. We never saw Him, never even heard His voice; He gave the white man laws but He had no word for His red children whose teeming millions filled this vast continent as the stars fill the firmament. No, we are two distinct races and must ever remain so. There is little in common between us. The ashes of our ancestors are sacred and the final resting place is hallowed ground, while you wander away from the tombs of your fathers seemingly without regret.

"Your religion was written on tables of stone by the iron finger of an angry God, lest you might forget it. The red man could never remember nor comprehend it. Our religion is the traditions of our ancestors, the dreams of our old men, given them by the Great Spirit, and the visions of our sachems, and is written in the hearts of our people.

"Your dead cease to love you and the homes of their nativity as soon as they pass the portals of the tomb. They wander far off beyond the stars, are soon forgotten and never return. Our dead never forget the beautiful world that gave them being. They still love its winding rivers, its great mountains and its sequestered vales, and they ever yearn in tenderest affection over the lonely-hearted living and often return to visit and comfort them.

"Day and night cannot dwell together. The red man has ever fled the approach of the white man, as the changing mists on the mountain side flee before the blazing morning sun.

"However your proposition seems a just one, and I think my folks will accept it and will retire to the reservation you offer them, and we will dwell apart and in peace, for the words of the great white chief seem to be the voice of nature speaking to my people out of the thick darkness that is fast gathering around them like a dense fog floating inward from a midnight sea.

"It matters but little where we pass the remainder of our days. They are not many. The Indian's night promises to be dark. No bright star hovers about the horizon. Sad-voiced winds moan in the distance. Some grim Nemesis of our race is on the red man's trail, and wherever he goes he will still hear the sure approaching footsteps of the fell destroyer and prepare to meet his doom, as does the wounded doe that hears the approaching footsteps of the hunter. A few more moons, a few more winters and not one of all the mighty hosts that once filled this broad land or that now roam in fragmentary bands through these vast solitudes will remain to weep over the tombs of a people once as powerful and as hopeful as your own.

"But why should we repine? Why should I murmur at the fate of my people? Tribes are made up of individuals and are no better than they. Men come and go like the waves of the sea. A tear, a *tamanamus*, a dirge, and they are gone from our longing eyes forever. Even the white man, whose God walks and talks with him as friend to friend, is not exempt from the common destiny. We *may* be brothers after all. We shall see.

"We will ponder your proposition, and when we have decided we will tell you. But should we accept it, I here and now make this the first condition: That we will not be denied the privilege, without molestation, of visiting at will the graves of our ancestors and friends.

"Every part of this country is sacred to my people. Every hillside, every valley, every plain and grove has been hallowed by some fond memory or some sad experience of my tribe. Even the rocks that seem to lie dumb as they swelter in the sun along the silent seashore in solemn grandeur thrill with memories of past events connected with the fate of my people, and the very dust under your feet responds more lovingly to our footsteps than to yours, because it is the ashes of our ancestors, and our bare feet are conscious of the sympathetic touch, for the soil is rich with the life of our kindred.

"The sable braves, and fond mothers and glad-hearted maidens, and the little children who lived and rejoiced here, and whose very names are now forgotten, still love these solitudes, and their deep fastnesses at eventide grow shadowy with the presence of dusky spirits. And when the last red man shall have perished from the earth and his memory among white men shall have become a myth, these shores shall swarm with the invisible dead of my tribe, and when your children's children shall think themselves alone in the field, the shop, upon the highway or in the silence of the woods they will not be alone.

"In all the earth there is no place dedicated to solitude. At night, when the streets of your cities and villages shall be silent, and you think them deserted, they will throng with the returning hosts that once filled and still love this beautiful land. The white man will never be alone. Let him be just and deal kindly with my people, for the dead are not altogether powerless."

Other speakers followed, but I took no notes. Governor Stevens's reply was brief. He merely promised to meet them in general council on some future occasion to discuss the proposed treaty. Chief Seattle's promise to adhere to the treaty, should one be ratified, was observed to the letter, for he was ever the unswerving and faithful friend of the white man. The above is but a fragment of his speech, and lacks all the charm lent by the grace and earnestness of the sable old orator and the occasion.

Following is another "Chief Seattle Address," written by Ted Perry in 1969 or 1970 for a film for the Southern Baptist Radio and Television Commission. In this rewrite, it is obvious (as in many of the so-called Chief Seattle addresses) that the original address has been heavily revised for a different time and a different audience. Nevertheless, it still speaks to us of the chief's deepest concerns and emphasizes the timeless importance of our respect and love for the Earth.

The Great Chief in Washington sends word that he wishes to buy our land. The Great Chief also sends us words of friendship and goodwill. This is kind of him, since we know he has little need of our friendship in return. But we will consider your offer. For we know that if we do not sell, the white man may come with guns and take our land.

How can you buy or sell the sky, the warmth of the land? The idea is strange to us. If we do not own the freshness of the air and the sparkle of the water, how can you buy them from us?

We will decide in our time. What Chief Seattle says, the Great Chief in Washington can count on as truly as our white brothers can count on the return of the seasons. My words are like the stars. They do not set.

Every part of this earth is sacred to my people. Every shining pine needle, every sandy shore, every mist in the dark woods, every clearing and humming insect is holy in the memory and experience of my people. The sap which courses through the trees carries the memories of the red man.

The white man's dead forget the country of their birth when they go to walk among the stars. Our dead never forget this beautiful earth, for it is the mother of the red man. We are part of the earth and it is part of us. The perfumed flowers are our sisters; the deer, the horse, the great eagle—these are our brothers. The rocky crests, the juices in the meadows, the body heat of the pony, and man—all belong to the same family.

So, when the Great Chief in Washington sends word that he wishes to buy our land, he asks much of us. The Great Chief sends word he will reserve us a place so that we can live comfortable to ourselves. He will be our father and we will be his children.

But can that ever be? God loves your people, but has abandoned his red children. He sends machines to help the white man with his work, and builds great villages for him. He makes your people stronger by the day. Soon you will flood the land like the rivers which crash down the canyons after a sudden rain. But my people are an ebbing tide, and we will never return. No, we are separate races. Our children do not play together and our old men tell different stories. God favors you, and we are orphans.

So we will consider your offer to buy our land. But it will not be easy. For this land is sacred to us. We take our pleasure in these woods. I do not know. Our ways are different from your ways.

This shining water that moves in the streams and rivers is not just water but the blood of our ancestors. If we sell you land, you must remember that it is sacred, and that each ghostly reflection in the clear water of the lakes tells of events and memories in the life of my people. The water's murmur is the voice of my father's father.

The rivers are our brothers—they quench our thirst. The rivers carry our canoes and feed our children. If we sell you our land, you must remember, and teach your children, that the rivers are our brothers, and yours, and you must henceforth give rivers the kindness you would give any brother.

The red man has always retreated before the advancing white man, as the mist of the mountain runs before the morning sun. But the ashes of our fathers are sacred. The graves are holy ground, and so these hills, these trees, this portion of the earth is consecrated to us.

We know that the white man does not understand our ways. One portion of the land is the same to him as the next, for he is a stranger who comes in the night and takes from the land whatever he needs. The earth is not his brother but his enemy, and when he has conquered it, he moves on. He leaves his father's graves behind, and he does not care. He kidnaps the earth from his children. He does not care. His father's graves and his children's birthright are forgotten. He treats his mother, the earth, and his brother, the sky, as things to be bought, plundered, and sold like sheep or bright beads. His appetite will devour the earth and leave behind only a desert.

I do not know. Our ways are different from your ways. The sight of your cities pains the eyes of the red man. But perhaps it is because the red man is a savage and does not understand. There is no quiet place in the white man's cities. No place to hear the unfurling of leaves in spring or the rustle of insect's wings. But perhaps it is because I am a savage and do not understand. The clatter only seems to insult the ears.

And what is there to life if a man cannot hear the lonely cry of the whippoorwill or the arguments of the frogs around a pond at night? I am a red man and do not understand. The Indian prefers the soft sound of the wind darting over the face of a pond, and the smell of the wind itself, cleansed by a midday rain, or scented with the piñon pine.

The air is precious to the red man, for all things share the same breath: the beast, the tree, the man—they all share the same breath. The white man does not seem to notice the air he breathes. Like a man dying for many days, he is numb to the stench. But if we sell our land, you must remember that the air is precious to us, that the air shares its spirit with all the life it supports. The wind that gave our grandfather his first breath also receives his last sigh. And the wind must also give our children the spirit of life. And if we sell you our land, you must keep it apart and sacred, as a place where even the white man can go to taste the wind that is sweetened by the meadow's flowers.

So we will consider your offer to buy our land. If we decide to accept, I will make one condition: The white man must treat the beasts of this land as his brothers. I am a savage and do not understand any other way. I have seen a thousand rotting buffalos on the prairie, left by the white man who shot them from a passing train. I am a savage and I do not understand how the smoking iron horse can be more important than the buffalo that we kill only to stay alive.

What is man without the beasts? If all the beasts were gone, men would die from a great loneliness of spirit. For whatever happens to the beasts, soon happens to man. All things are connected. Whatever befalls the earth, befalls the sons of the earth.

You must teach your children that the ground beneath their feet is the ashes of our grandfathers. So that they will respect the land, tell your children that the earth is rich with the lives of our kin. Teach your children what we have taught our children, that the earth is our mother. Whatever befalls the earth, befalls the sons of the earth. If men spit upon the ground, they spit upon themselves.

This we know: The earth does not belong to man; man belongs to the earth. This we know: All things are connected like the blood which unites one family. All things are connected. Whatever befalls the earth befalls the sons of the earth. Man did not weave the web of life; he is merely a strand in it. Whatever he does to the web, he does to himself.

No, day and night cannot live together. Our dead go to live in the earth's sweet rivers, they return with the silent footsteps of spring, and it is their spirit, running in the wind, that ripples the surface of the ponds.

We will consider why the white man wishes to buy the land. What is it that the white man wishes to buy, my people ask me. The idea is strange to us. How can you buy or sell the sky, the warmth of the land, the swiftness of the antelope? How can we sell these things to you and how can you buy them? Is the earth yours to do with as you will, merely because the red man signs a piece of paper and gives it to the white man? If we do not own the freshness of the air and sparkle of the water, how can you buy them from us? Can you buy back the buffalo, once the last one has been killed?

But we will consider your offer, for we know that if we do not sell, the white man may come with guns and take our land. We are primitive, and in his passing moment of strength the white man thinks that he is a god who already owns the earth. How can a man own his mother? But we will consider your offer to buy our land.

Day and night cannot live together. We will consider your offer to go to the reservation you have for my people. We will live apart, and in peace. It matters little where we spend the rest of our days. Our children have seen their fathers humbled in defeat. Our warriors have felt shame, and after defeat they turn their days in idleness and contaminate their bodies with sweet foods and strong drink.

It matters little where we pass the rest of our days. They are not many. A few more hours, a few more winters, and none of the children of the great tribes that once lived on this earth or that roam now in small bands in the woods will be left to mourn the graves of a people once as powerful and hopeful as yours.

But why should I mourn the passing of my people? Tribes are made of men, nothing more. Men come and go, like the waves of the sea. Even the white man, whose God walks and talks with him as friend to friend, cannot be exempt from the common destiny. We may be brothers after all. We shall see.

One thing we know, which the white man may one day discover: Our God is the same God. You may think now that you own Him as you wish to own our land; but you cannot. He is the God of man, and His compassion is equal for the red man and the white. This earth is precious to Him, and to harm the earth is to heap contempt on its Creator. The whites too shall pass, perhaps sooner than all other tribes. Continue to contaminate your bed, and you will one night suffocate in your own waste.

But in your perishing you will shine brightly, fired by the strength of the God who brought you to this land and for some special purpose gave you dominion over this land and over the red man. That destiny is a mystery do us, for we do not understand when the buffalo are all slaughtered, the wild horses are tamed, the secret corners of the forest heavy with the scent of many men, and the view of the ripe hills blotted by talking wires. Where is the thicket? Gone. Where is the eagle. Gone. And what is it to say goodbye to the swift pony and the hunt? The end of living and the beginning of survival.

God gave you dominion over the beasts, the woods, and the red man, and for some special purpose, but that destiny is a mystery to the red man. We might understand if we knew what it was that the white man dreams—what hopes he describes to his children on long winter nights, what visions he burns onto their minds so that they will wish for tomorrow. But we are savages. The white man's dreams are hidden from us. And because they are hidden, we will go our own way. For above all else, we cherish the right of each man to live as he wishes, however different from his brothers. There is little in common between us.

So we will consider your offer to buy our land. If we agree, it will be to secure the reservation you have promised. There, perhaps, we may live out our brief days as we wish.

When the last red man has vanished from this earth, and his memory is only the shade of a cloud moving across the prairie, these shores and forests will still behold the spirits of my people. For they love this earth as the newborn loves its mother's heartbeat.

If we sell you our land, love it as we have loved it. Care for it as we have cared for it. Hold in your mind the memory of the land as it is when you take it. And with all your strength, with all your mind, with all your heart, preserve it for your children, and love it . . . as God loves us all.

One thing we know: Our God is the same God. This earth is precious to Him. Even the white man cannot be exempt from the common destiny. We may be brothers after all. We shall see.

2. Series of quotes taken from a compilation entitled "Cross-Cultural Exchange and Prophetic Tradition: The Hopi and Tibetan Dialogue," by Joan Price.

3. Thomas Francis Tarbet, ed., *From the Beginning of Life to the Day of Purification*, 3d ed. (Taos, NM: Hopi Land and Life, 1982). Reprinted with permission from Hopi Land and Life, a constituent member of Taos Learning Centers, Inc., and from the Planting Stick Project, Rte. 9, Box 78, Santa Fe, NM 87505.

4. Reprinted from *The Hopi Hearings, July 15-30, 1955*, Bureau of Indian Affairs, Phoenix Area Office, Keams Canyon, AZ.

5. Bronislaw Malinowski, *Myth in Primitive Psychology*, as quoted in *The Larousse World Mythology*, ed. Pierre Grimal (Secaucus, NJ: Chartwell Books, 1973), 12.

6. Leonard Cottrell, *The Horizon Book of Lost Worlds* (New York: American Heritage Publishing Co., 1962), 46.

7. *The Larousse World Mythology*, 475.

8. Frank Waters, *Mexico Mystique* (Chicago: Swallow Press, 1975).

9. Frank Waters, *Book of the Hopi* (New York: The Viking Press, 1963).

10. L. Taylor Hansen, *He Walked the Americas* (Amherst, WI: Amherst Press, 1963).

11. It has been said that the banana plant was introduced to the American continent by the invading Spaniards. I personally disagree with this concept. In fact, there is a good body of evidence supporting the belief that earlier settlers brought the plant from Asia—possibly Java, Sumatra, Borneo, or Indochina. Moreover, the banana is not common in Spain. It is also known that Polynesian groups brought the banana to Easter Island (a thousand miles off the coast of Chile) more than a thousand years before the settlement of Mesoamerica by the Spaniards. It makes more sense that it reached the mainland and Mesoamerica through one of these channels than through the hands of Spanish conquerors and immigrants.

ABOUT THE AUTHOR

Robert Boissière has had close ties with the Native American world for the past forty years. Born and raised in France, he first went to Hopiland in northern Arizona in 1949 and stayed with the Koyawena family, establishing a relationship that has continued through the present, ever deepening his understanding of the Hopi way of life.

During a visit to Taos Pueblo in New Mexico in 1952, he met Mary Santanita (Po Pai Mo), who was to become his wife. They lived at the pueblo until Mary's untimely death in 1958. Since this tragic event, his frequent contacts with Pueblo cultures have had great impact on his life and beliefs.

Boissière brings a rich background to *The Return of Pahana*. His French cultural heritage, his knowledge of Native American ways, and extensive travel in Peru, Bolivia, and the Yucatán have all contributed to his comprehensive understanding of the planetary myth of the return of a supernatural archetype, which is the subject of the book.

The Return of Pahana is Boissière's fourth book. His first, *Po Pai Mo: The Search for White Buffalo Woman*, was published in 1983 by Sunstone Press in Santa Fe, New Mexico. This autobiography was followed by two books in close succession: *The Hopi Way*, published by Sunstone in 1985, and *Meditations with the Hopi*, published by Bear & Company in 1986.